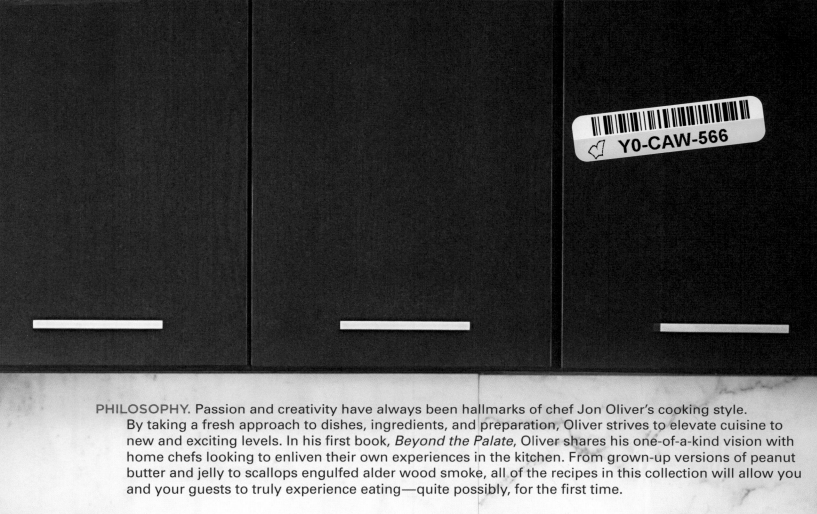

PHILOSOPHY. Passion and creativity have always been hallmarks of chef Jon Oliver's cooking style. By taking a fresh approach to dishes, ingredients, and preparation, Oliver strives to elevate cuisine to new and exciting levels. In his first book, *Beyond the Palate*, Oliver shares his one-of-a-kind vision with home chefs looking to enliven their own experiences in the kitchen. From grown-up versions of peanut butter and jelly to scallops engulfed alder wood smoke, all of the recipes in this collection will allow you and your guests to truly experience eating—quite possibly, for the first time.

Would you like to experience Chef Oliver's unique culinary artistry in your own kitchen? Make a reservation at **www.thepersonalpalate.com**.

To Arlene —

Experience Food!

Chef

by **chef jon oliver**

BEYOND THE PALATE

palate \pa-lət\ *n.* **1.** the roof of the mouth. **2.** the sense of taste.
palatable \pa-lə-tə-bəl\ *adj.* **1.** appetizing, savory, agreeable, or pleasant to the sense of taste.

NORTHSTAR MEDIA

Publisher
Northstar Books, LLC

Text and Recipes by
Jon Oliver

Text copyright © 2010
Jon Oliver

Chef Assistant
Patrick Whetstone

Writer/Editor
Evan West

Creative Director
Kathy Davis

Photographers
Portrait photography Copyright
© 2010 Charles Park
Location and Food photography by
Stacy Newgent

Cover image: Grilled Cheese &
Tomato Soup (recipe on page 30),
by Stacy Newgent

Library of Congress Catalog-in-
Publication Data available.

ISBN: 978-0-9820296-6-4

Printed in Singapore

10 9 8 7 6 5 4 3 2 1

Northstar Books, LLC
120 East Vermont Street
Indianapolis, IN 46204

www.northstarmediabooks.com

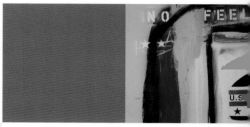

CONTENTS

to my family

THIS BOOK IS DEDICATED TO MY WONDERFUL WIFE, PAIGE—FOR HER LOVE, SUPPORT, AND ENCOURAGEMENT; AND TO MY SONS—AVISTON AND CORRICK. MAY THEY GROW TO HAVE THEIR OWN PASSIONS IN LIFE AND ALWAYS KNOW THAT THEIR MOM AND I LOVE THEM BOTH DEARLY.

the calling

FOOD IS A VAST WORLD. IT'S NOT SOMETHING YOU CAN MASTER, AND THAT'S WHAT DRAWS ME TO IT.

SOME PEOPLE ARE FRUSTRATED BY THE FACT THAT THEY will never know everything about their chosen profession. However, for me it's a real comfort. As a chef, I relish the fact that there is an endless variety of cuisine from around the globe. There are ingredients and cooking techniques that some chefs have never seen or heard of. There are probably things in the ocean yet to discover. Exploring the expansive, diverse realm that is food is a big driver for me, and I love that I will never know all there is to know about it. If you are a person who constantly strives to learn something new and spin that knowledge with creativity, then cooking may be in your blood.

Another aspect of being a chef that drives my passion: It is not something that everyone can do. A lot of people can't think of food as anything more than fuel. They would never pay for a multi-course meal, let alone cook for a living, because they can't accept the fact that there is beauty in something you're

simply going to eat. But I see eating as something more. It is one of the few things in life that is experienced every day, and it is intertwined in the lives of every person on the planet. I get a tremendous amount of satisfaction from taking something ordinary like eating and pushing it to an extraordinary level. Food might just be fuel, but when I make it I want to blow your doors off. Some people like to say that "anybody can cook." But can anybody turn cooking into an art form? For me, being a chef is more than a career; it is a calling. I get to wake up every day and do what I was born to do.

I didn't realize that food was my passion until well after I had graduated from high school. Don't get me wrong: It's not like my family went hungry when I was a kid. When I was growing up, my grandpa kept his garden on our property in Warsaw, Indiana. Every single day, all summer long, he would drive over at 6 o'clock in the morning to start planting, watering, and

7

weeding. He was always bringing buckets of tomatoes and cucumbers up to the house, so we had plenty of fresh vegetables around. Still, there was a world of cooking that we Olivers knew nothing about. My dad would spend the money to buy T-bone steaks and then grill the heck out of them. I didn't even know what medium-rare was until I was in high school.

But looking back, I can see plenty of signs that I had a special connection with food even at an early age. One of my most vivid memories is of a science fair project that I completed in elementary school. I got the idea to explore the relationship between the nose and the taste buds, and I designed an experiment where I held things under people's noses while I fed them food that was fairly neutral in flavor. I then observed how the smells influenced how the food tasted. The project, which I called "Is one sniff worth a thousand tastes?" ended up winning a blue ribbon. I don't have many memories of math or other subjects from school, but that experience is crystal clear in my mind. Interestingly enough, linking the different senses, particularly taste and smell, is something I emphasize in my cooking today.

I was the youngest of six kids, so a lot of times I had to fend for myself in the kitchen. I'd come down for breakfast and my brother would be eating cereal out of the box. At one point, my sister used a bran muffin recipe from the back of a cereal box, and after that I started making muffins all the time. Later, my dad showed me how to make a 90-second egg using the microwave. Before long, I was onto frying pans and cooking up a little bacon while my brother and sisters were still eating cold cereal. Eventually, I found out that I could barter with food. I would be making an egg sandwich, and my brother would come up and say, "Man, that looks good." So I would offer to make him a sandwich if he agreed to take out the trash for a week. Cooking was opening doors for me even then.

I GOT MY FIRST JOB, AT AN ARBY'S RESTAURANT, WHEN I was 15. I had no idea that working with food was what I wanted to do in life; I just wanted to make money. It was hard to get passionate about slopping roast beef around all day. Before it was roasted, the meat came to the restaurant in a big, flat, heavy plastic bag. One time, I thought it would be fun to turn the thing into a punching bag, Rocky Balboa style. The manager wasn't too happy when he caught me doing that. All in all, I had just as much fun mopping the floors, and I was more interested in goofing around than I was working with the food. Let's just say I didn't take the job too seriously. When I saw how much money my brother was making working at the car wash, I bolted for greener pastures. "The money is not in cooking," I thought.

As my high school graduation neared, my mom asked me, "So, what do you want to do?" To tell you the truth, I had never given it much thought. I was doing pretty well at the car wash, and it wasn't like there was college money just sitting there for me. Even though my Arby's experience hadn't made much of an impression on me, it occurred to me how much I enjoyed making food at home. "Maybe I'll pursue this cooking thing," I thought. "I kind of have a knack for it." Granted, I was basing this off of making eggs and bacon. My parents had a friend who was a chef, and they arranged for me to meet with him. "Jon," he told me. "It's great that you're interested in cooking, but let me give you a huge piece of advice: Do not go to

9

THERE IS SOMETHING SO TRUE ABOUT THE MAXIM, A PLACE FOR EVERYTHING, AND EVERYTHING IN ITS PLACE.

culinary school until you've worked in a real restaurant, because there is a world of difference between cooking as a hobby and being passionate enough about it to want to cook for a living."

My mom had bought me a membership at a local country club as a graduation present, and the club had a restaurant called Orion's. I thought I would take the advice of my parents' chef friend and try getting a job there. It turned out they were hiring a prep cook/dishwasher. The chef/owner of the restaurant was this big burly guy named Kurt Samuelson, and he sat me down, looked at me, and said, "Jon, cooking isn't easy. It's hard work. There's a lot I can show you, but you will probably never be as good as me." Those words are still braised into my head. It was a challenge. I figured if I was never going to know as much as he did, I would at least try to learn as much as I could. This was my first stop. "I'll see your prep cook job," I told him, "and I'll raise you as much as I can possibly learn."

So he gave me a shot. Within a year and a half, I had blown through the prep cook job, worked as a line cook, and, finally, had taken over as sous chef. Kurt gave me a salary of less than $20,000 a year, which, at the time, was more than I thought I would ever make in my whole life. He worked my butt into the ground, but I was thankful. There I was, 20 years old, employed as a sous chef at a country club for a chef who knew more than anyone else in the world. I thought I had arrived.

At Orion's, we had a big iron skillet, and that thing blazed all day and all night. If you didn't turn it on when you got there at 9 A.M., it wasn't going to be hot enough by noon. We probably blackened every single piece of meat there was to blacken. I used that skillet to create what would become my first signature dish. We served prime rib on Friday and Saturday nights, and we would end up with a bunch of leftover meat. I said, "Why don't we slice it, pile it up, blacken both sides, throw it on a sandwich bun, and put Monterey Jack cheese on it? We can call it the Black Jack." We served it for lunch throughout the week, and that thing sold like gangbusters. From then on, I was known as the guy who invented the Black Jack sandwich. It was my first taste of being famous, and from then on, creativity and inventiveness would come to define my approach as a chef.

I MARRIED MY GORGEOUS WIFE, PAIGE, IN 1997, WHILE I was still working at Orion's. I left Orion's and moved to Indianapolis to live with her while she attended the University of Indianapolis, and I took a job as a cook at the Adam's Mark hotel. After about a year and a half, I was promoted to sous chef, and I pretty much did it all: fine-dining, banquets, and even ice-carving. Two of the chefs I worked for, executive chef Ray Wilson and executive sous chef Allen Gustin, had attended culinary school at Johnson & Wales University, and they were on me all the time to follow suit. "Oliver, you need to go to school," they would tell me. "You're good, but you need to get even better." So when my wife finished her degree, that's what I did. I enrolled at Johnson & Wales in Charleston, South Carolina, and my wife and I moved down there. I finished my entire two-year degree in 11 months, including a 10-week internship at The Grove Park Inn Resort & Spa in Asheville,

North Carolina. I arrived there right before Mother's Day, in 2001. They did a massive Mother's Day brunch, and a week before the big day the freezer went down; all of the ice carvings they had finished were ruined. The guy who normally did the ice carving also did all the garde manger, or cold pantry section, so he needed help. "We need 30 blocks of ice cut," he told me, "and you've got one week." So I knocked them out. From then on, whenever I walked through the resort, people would yell out, "The Iceman cometh!" Once again, I was famous. I hadn't taken my internship with the intention of carving ice, but it turned out to be my lucky break. After I saved the day, they said I could spend the rest of my internship doing whatever I wanted. So I told them I wanted to work at Horizons, the resort's fine-dining restaurant. They told me no interns ever work at Horizons, but they agreed to let me try it for two weeks. Well, the chef loved having me around, and I got to work there for the rest of my internship, which gave me an excellent grounding in high-end cuisine.

When my internship was over, my wife got a good job back in Indianapolis, and I returned ready to resume my career. I signed on as a sous chef at the University Place Conference Center & Hotel, on the campus of IUPUI, and my assignment was to transform Chancellor's Restaurant into an award-winning eatery. We made a good run at it, and I helped create a level of food they hadn't seen before. Things were rolling. One of my goals had been to be an executive chef by the time I was 30. University Place promoted me to executive chef of the hotel at the age of 29. I had come a long way

since my days at Arby's in Warsaw. I had achieved what I set out to do.

SO IN 2006, WHEN LIFE PRESENTED ME WITH ANOTHER opportunity, I was ready to seize it. That was the year my wife became pregnant with our first child. After nine years of marriage, no kids, and the freedom to do whatever we wanted career-wise, we had to figure out how having a family would change the status quo. What did we want our lives to be like when our child arrived? Did we want to do day care from sunup to sundown, or should one of us stay at home? After we went over the numbers, it didn't take a rocket scientist to figure out that Paige should not quit her job. She never got phone calls at 4 o'clock in the morning informing her that she had to go into the hotel to get breakfast going. I loved the cooking part of being a chef at the hotel, but I wasn't crazy about what I deemed the "reality" part. I was working like a mule, sometimes 70 to 80 hours a week, and that wasn't something I would miss.

I had to figure out how I could be a stay-at-home dad while also doing what I loved. So I sat down and made a of list of everything I loved to do, and thought about how I could combine those things. I wanted to be able to cook high-end food. I also knew that I really enjoyed interacting with diners. And I liked the instructional aspect of being a chef, which involved sharing my knowledge of food with others. Putting all those elements together gave rise to the concept for **The Personal Palate**, which provides private, personalized,

ESTABLISHED
1806

in-home dining experiences for clients who wish to employ my services.

With The Personal Palate, I think I've created a business model that fills a very special niche. You only have to turn on the television to see that chefs are hot personalities right now, and everybody seems to want to get a glimpse into that lifestyle. The Personal Palate gives my clients an opportunity to do just that, in their own home. With the clients' input, I design a customized, multi-course dinner menu that I prepare in their kitchen and serve to their guests, along with pairings of high-end beverages. All the client has to do at the event is relax, sit back, and kick it, while we make them look like rock stars.

Sometimes, when people are planning an event, they call me and say, "I heard you were doing some catering." When someone starts a phone conversation that way, I have to ask them: "What do you mean by catering?" If they're throwing a party for 40, and they need chicken salad on croissants and some bags of chips, I tell them they need to call someone else. I am very honest with my clients: The Personal Palate is not a catering company. We are the entertainment of the night. We do high-end, food-driven events. We take food and beverage, bring it to you at as high a level as you want it (often my dinner parties are less expensive than taking a group out to a fine-dining restaurant), and then blow you out of your chair. We can make a meal last for three hours. And it's an experience you're going to talk about for the next 20 years.

THE PERSONAL PALATE HAS TURNED OUT TO BE THE perfect fit for my family and me, because it meets all of the needs I set out to fulfill. It gives me the flexibility to spend time with them, and yet continue my passion for making great food. I have a close personal connection with my clients, and, if they're interested, I get to teach them a thing or two about cooking along the way. When I launched The Personal Palate, I told God, "It's not really my business, it's Yours. If You want to bless it, You bless it." And that's what He has done.

THE TANTALIZING AROMA OF SMOKE AND SEAFOOD (LEFT).

17

As I have said before, this is more than just work for me. I feel like being a chef is what God has called me to do. After all these years working as a chef, my conviction that I was called to make food is stronger than ever. There has never been a day when I woke up and thought, "I never want to cook again." If a million dollars fell from the sky right now, I'd still be in the kitchen later tonight. I just love food. And that love stems, in part, from the artistic side of what I do, and the satisfaction I get from the process. I think most artists aren't truly happy until they actually find a home for what they've created. If I were a painter, it would take me weeks or months to finish a canvas, and it might take even longer to sell it. But as a chef, I get instant gratification. When I'm in a client's home, I get to have a lot of fun making the food, and then I get to be there while it is enjoyed. There's something exciting about how quickly the process moves. Food is a moment in time. Once you eat it, it's gone forever. And if you weren't at the dinner party, you missed it.

PAIRINGS OF PREMIUM WINE AND BEER ARE AN IMPORTANT PART OF THE PERSONAL PALATE EXPERIENCE.

how to use this book

RULES TO PLAY BY. This book is about 2 things: loving to cook and loving to eat good cooking. I approach cooking like art, and being creative is a big part of what I enjoy about it. But another important factor in my style is understanding some of the science behind the food. I like to know how ingredients interact with one another, and why different techniques and processes yield different results. In fact, for me, the creativity only comes after a basic understanding of what happens to food on a chemical and biological level when it is prepared. Getting to know more about the nature of ingredients and techniques allows me to explode my cooking onto a whole new level. I know that if I do x, the result will be y. That gets my mind working in all kinds of exciting directions. "What is happening now? What will happen if I do this, or that?" Those are questions I ask myself as I cook.

I am fortunate because my wife happens to have degrees in biology and chemistry. As I wrote in the previous section, I consider being a chef a calling. Similarly, I think my wife and I ended up together for a reason, and one of the reasons is that her expertise is a perfect compliment to my passion for cooking. She is like my back-pocket scientist. When I have questions about why certain things work and why others don't, I can bounce them off of her. When I first learned how to make stocks from other chefs, they would say, "Put this and that in there, fill it with water, then turn on the heat." But no one ever taught me why in the heck we were doing that. When I was in culinary school, I got to study textbooks from my wife's college science courses, and I could look up which proteins were water-soluble and which ones weren't, then convert that knowledge into making stocks. On the other hand, I know that acid can denature a protein, so if I put lime juice on fish, I can figure out how much lime juice to use and how long it should remain for a desired effect.

Of course, I don't expect you to understand all of the complex chemical and biological processes of cooking after reading this book. In fact, I don't think anyone can learn it all; there's just too much. Instead, I want to offer a glimpse into the kind of creative processes that go into my cooking. And I hope that some of the following "rules" will enhance your enjoyment of cooking and make your experience using this book more rewarding.

TEMPERATURE. First and foremost, note that all of the cooking temperatures outlined in the following recipes are measured in degrees Fahrenheit. In most of the recipes, the word "Fahrenheit" has been omitted to avoid repetition.

KEEP AN OPEN MIND. The recipes in a lot of cook books are broken into the parts of a meal with a traditional progression, such as starters, soups, salads, and so on. But I don't really approach food using those traditional divisions. When I prepare a meal, I think of each dish as an individual course of food, each roughly the same size, with no one course more important than the others. Where each course falls in the meal isn't dictated by tradition, such as serving a "starter" course first. Instead, the order of the courses is determined by what I think is a natural progression. A course might have a salad component, but that doesn't mean it has to be served early in the meal; it might depend on what other courses I'm serving, or what will facilitate a good progression in the beverages that accompany them.

So instead of organizing my recipe chapters into traditional courses, I wanted to use unique concepts that give the reader a feel for how my mind works when I am creating new dishes. One thing I'm passionate about is making food fun and memorable, and one way to do that is to play off of familiar items that people have had a hundred times, but make sure it will be a unique experience when I serve it to them. In the "Childhood Memories" chapter, for example, I'm taking dishes that nearly everyone remembers from childhood and giving them a more sophisticated, grown-up twist. For a novel approach to peanut butter and jelly, I asked myself, "What's something unique I can do with this?" Instantly, I thought of Thai peanut sauce, which I love. Then I thought, "Why can't peanut butter and jelly be spicy?" So I came up with red chili jam, because red chili peppers are common in Thai cuisine. It also occurred to me that I liked peanut butter on crackers, but to stay with the Asian theme I used a wonton. This is how my brain works in the kitchen. The result was my recipe for Spicy Thai Peanut Butter, Red Chili Jam, Wonton Crisp (page 26). I hope using a playful, innovative approach to organizing the recipes in this book will trigger creativity in your cooking as well.

SEEK BALANCE. I conceived and wrote the book in a way that would reflect my personal style, which generally involves making several elaborate dishes in a multi-course setting. So if you want to fabricate what I do by making an entire recipe as described in this book, that's great. But if you want to use only individual components from within the recipes, there are some ground rules you should consider. When I designed these recipes, the character of each component was intended to compliment and balance the flavors and textures of all the other components in the dish. So if you pull one component out and serve it by itself, it might be missing an element that I included in another component. For instance, in the recipe for Shellfish Shooters (page 76), I created an avocado soup that goes under a lump crab ceviche, which is then topped by a lime vinaigrette. If you just want to make the avocado soup and serve it by itself, keep in mind that the acidity is actually coming from the lime vinaigrette, and there is heat coming from the jalapeno salt I use to rim the shot glass. So you might want to add some lime and jalapenos; otherwise, you will be missing the whole picture.

SIZE UP THE PORTIONS. Because I approach each dish in this book as an individual course of food, the portion sizes yielded by most recipes will be roughly the same. I tend to approach my courses in this way in order to make them appropriate for a multi-course, tasting-style dinner, because I don't want to fill up my diners on any one course. Don't feel like you have to make every component in a given recipe, but if you do decide to single out one item, keep in mind that the portion size and number of servings detailed in the recipe are geared toward a multi-course style of meal. Let's say that you want to throw down a rib dinner for the whole family, so you decide to make the Slow-Braised Short Ribs (page 112). The recipe calls for 4 pounds of boneless short ribs and is intended to serve 10 to 12 people in a multi-course meal. If you were serving 10 people, that would be about 6 ounces of ribs per person, which might not be enough if you're not serving a bunch of other courses. So if you have a few big eaters who want to eat a pound of meat per person, you might want to bulk up on the ribs.

HAVE PATIENCE. The great French chef Auguste Escoffier is credited with creating what are known as the "mother sauces," one of which is the velouté (or "velvet"), made from chicken stock. If you go to any chef in the business right now, he could probably whip up a velouté sauce in 15 or 20 minutes. But Escoffier said that a proper velouté requires two hours of simmering, minimum. I would encourage anyone to try making a 20-minute velouté and a two-hour velouté, then tell me which one more closely resembles velvet. There's just

METICULOUS PLATING YIELDS BEAUTIFUL RESULTS.

something to be said for time. There is no substitute for it. I am a patient chef because I understand that good things come to those who wait.

I have some very simple recipes that can be duplicated quickly, but I also have recipes that take longer to make. And you will be rewarded if you spend the time to make them correctly. Cooking is a process, and the process is part of the fun. Back to the example of the Slow-Braised Short Ribs: They need to be in the oven for about four hours. It's not like you have to mess with them continuously that whole time; get them going well enough in advance and they'll be done in time for dinner. But you can't just come home from work and whip them up. It's natural to look for shortcuts, and people often want to know if they can combine steps in a recipe, or go from step one to step five and still get the same end result. Well, I probably included steps two, three, and four for a reason. You may find a shortcut in there someplace after you understand the process, but do so at your own risk.

BE CREATIVE. My intention with this book is not just to give you a collection of Jon Oliver recipes to duplicate in your kitchen. I also want to give you a glimpse of how I approach food, and help open a wide creative window through which you can look at your own cooking in a new way. I hope some of the ideas and suggestions in this book will spark you to try new ingredients and techniques in your cooking, even when you are not making one of my recipes. Most people are familiar with onion and garlic powder, for instance. But it doesn't have to stop there. I have included a recipe for making a tomato powder (Mac & Goat Cheese, page 34). What else can you make into a powder? The sky's the limit. With a dehydrator and a coffee grinder, you can make almost anything into a powder—mushrooms, peppers, herbs, anything. The next thing you know, you're making your own signature grill seasonings. Don't be afraid to take ideas from this book and run with them.

BUY THE TOOLS IF YOU'RE GOING TO USE THEM. Chefs love toys, and I'm no different. I recommend some highly specialized tools throughout the book. The recipe for Fish and Chips (page 38) calls for using a rolling net cutter, which creates a cool net pattern out of thinly sliced vegetables. But it would be crazy for you to invest in one of those if you were just going to make a potato net for this one recipe. If you're going to buy it, consider all the other applications and presentations you could use it for. When you start thinking about the cool possibilities that open up once you have the tool, there's really no end to it.

RELAX. The photos in this book are a tribute to how much I love food. Many of the dishes are elaborately presented in the photos because I get as much enjoyment from plating food as I do making it. I opted to present the food creatively because I think of myself as an artist. This is what I do. But I don't want you to be intimidated by the presentations. Most of these dishes would look great plated a hundred different ways. I don't trace a line when I drizzle something, or draw up a map when I place a garnish. I just use a natural movement, and the ingredients fall how they fall. I think of a plate as a canvas. When you are plating, I would encourage you just to have fun with it. You will find a way to incorporate your own unique style and personality. Make it your own.

childhood memories

I INCLUDED THIS CHAPTER TO HONOR THE FOOD I USED TO EAT WHEN I WAS A KID. YOU MIGHT CALL THESE RECIPES HIGH-END VERSIONS OF KIDDIE FOOD.

A CHILD'S UNDEVELOPED PALATE IS MUCH DIFFERENT than an adult's, so most kids' food is simplified to some extent. I wanted to take that simplistic food and elevate it to a level that makes it enjoyable for grown-ups. One of my takes on P, B & J, for example, uses pistachio butter instead of peanut butter. Instead of plain old grape jelly, we're making chardonnay honey. And forget the Wonder bread; we're baking artisanal raisin bread into tasty crisps. I ate a lot of peanut butter and jelly when I was a kid, and you probably did, too. But I bet you've never had peanut butter

and jelly quite like this. One of my passions is to enhance the experience of food by connecting the diner to past memories. It's like looking through a window in time that begs the question, "Do you remember when...?" The concept of 'childhood memories' is also a good introduction to my style of cooking, because it shows how I take a familiar dish and turn it into a new and exciting creation.

"i take a
familiar
dish
and turn
it into a
new and
exciting
creation."

pb & j

SPICY THAI PEANUT BUTTER, RED CHILI JAM, WONTON CRISPS
ALMOND BUTTER, BING CHERRY AMARETTO PRESERVES, DARK CHOCOLATE TUILES
PISTACHIO BUTTER, CHARDONNAY HONEY, RAISIN CRISP
SERVES 8

SPICY THAI PEANUT BUTTER, RED CHILI JAM, WONTON CRISP

THAI PEANUT BUTTER

YIELDS 2 CUPS

3 CUPS DRY ROASTED PEANUTS
1 TEASPOON KOSHER SALT
1 TEASPOON HONEY
1 1/2 TABLESPOONS PEANUT OIL
1/2 TEASPOON CAYENNE PEPPER
1 TABLESPOON SOY SAUCE
1/2 TEASPOON LIME ZEST
1 TEASPOON LIME JUICE
1 TEASPOON MINCED GARLIC
1/2 TEASPOON MINCED GINGER

1. Place the peanuts, salt, and honey in the bowl of a food processor. Process for 1 minute.
2. Scrape down the sides of the bowl. With the lid on, continue to process while slowly drizzling in the oil; process until the mixture is smooth (about 1 1/2-2 minutes).
3. Blend in the remaining ingredients. Place in an airtight container and store in the refrigerator for up to 2 months.

RED CHILI JAM

12 FRESH MEDIUM-HOT FRESNO CHILIES
2 SMALL LEMONS, QUARTERED
1/2 CUP CIDER VINEGAR
. 3 CUPS GRANULATED SUGAR

1. Stem, seed, and finely chop the chilies.
2. In a small pot over medium heat, combine the chilies, lemons, and vinegar and simmer until the chilies are tender (about 30 minutes).
3. Remove the lemon quarters and add the sugar; raise the heat to medium high and boil until the jam reaches and passes the sheeting test (about 10 minutes).*

WONTON CRISPS

4 CUPS CANOLA OIL
10 WONTON WRAPPERS
SALT, TO TASTE

1. In a stockpot, bring the oil to 350 degrees over medium heat. The oil should be less than halfway up the inside of pot to prevent splattering.
2. Fry the wonton wrappers 1 at a time until they are crisp (about 30 seconds).
3. Remove them to a paper towel-lined pan and season to taste with salt.

ALMOND BUTTER, BING CHERRY AMARETTO PRESERVES, DARK CHOCOLATE TUILES

ALMOND BUTTER

YIELDS ¾ CUP

1 CUP SHELLED ALMONDS
¼ TEASPOON SEA SALT
1 TABLESPOON VEGETABLE OIL

1. Preheat oven to 325 degrees.
2. Spread the almonds on a sheet pan and roast in the oven for 20 minutes, stirring occasionally to ensure even roasting.
3. Combine the almonds and salt in a food processor, blender, meat grinder, or nut butter machine and process until the nuts are finely ground.
4. Add the oil and continue processing until the almond butter reaches your desired degree of smoothness, adding more oil if necessary. The almond butter should be smooth and spreadable.

BING CHERRY AMARETTO PRESERVES

2 CUPS PITTED BING CHERRIES
3 CUPS GRANULATED SUGAR
1 TEASPOON LEMON JUICE
1 TEASPOON POWDERED PECTIN
¼ CUP WATER
⅔ CUP AMARETTO

1. Combine the cherries, sugar, and lemon juice. Let stand for 20 minutes, stirring occasionally.
2. In a small saucepan, combine the pectin, water, and amaretto.
3. Bring to a rolling boil and boil for 1 minute, stirring constantly.
4. Add the cherry mixture to the pectin mixture; stir for 3 minutes. Remove from heat and let cool.

pb & j

SPICY THAI PEANUT BUTTER, RED CHILI JAM, WONTON CRISP
ALMOND BUTTER, BING CHERRY AMARETTO PRESERVES, DARK CHOCOLATE TUILES
PISTACHIO BUTTER, CHARDONNAY HONEY, RAISIN CRISP
SERVES 8

DARK CHOCOLATE TUILES

YIELDS 1 1/2 CUP OF BATTER

6 TABLESPOONS UNSALTED BUTTER
1/2 CUP PLUS 1 TABLESPOON GRANULATED SUGAR
3 EGG WHITES
1 TEASPOON VANILLA EXTRACT
1/4 CUP PLUS 1 TABLESPOON ALL-PURPOSE FLOUR
1/4 CUP UNSWEETENED COCOA POWDER

1. Preheat oven to 425 degrees.
2. In a mixing bowl, cream the butter and sugar together.
3. Gradually incorporate the egg whites and vanilla.
4. In a separate bowl, sift the flour with the cocoa powder.
5. Add the flour mixture to the sugar paste and mix just until the ingredients are incorporated.
6. Line 2 baking sheets (as needed) with silicone baking mats.
7. Spread the paste evenly and thinly on the silicone baking sheets and then bake for approximately 8 minutes. Use stencils, if desired.**
8. Remove from the oven and, if desired, shape cookies while they're warm; or, once cookies have cooled, they can be broken and served.

PISTACHIO BUTTER, CHARDONNAY HONEY, RAISIN CRISP

PISTACHIO BUTTER

YIELDS 1 1/2 CUPS

2 CUPS SHELLED PISTACHIOS
1 TEASPOON KOSHER SALT
2 TABLESPOONS HONEY
4 TABLESPOONS OLIVE OIL

1. Place the pistachios, salt, and honey in the bowl of a food processor and then process for 1 minute.
2. Scrape down the sides of the bowl. With the lid on, continue to process while slowly drizzling in the oil; process until the mixture is smooth (1 1/2-2 minutes).

CHARDONNAY HONEY

1 BOTTLE (750 ML) CHARDONNAY
1/2 CUP TURBINADO SUGAR

1. In a heavy saucepan over medium-low heat, reduce the chardonnay to 1 cup.
2. Add the sugar and continue reducing over low heat until syrup forms (about 10 minutes).
3. Cool and adjust thickness with water if necessary.

RAISIN CRISP

1 LOAF QUALITY RAISIN BREAD (ARTISAN STYLE)†
1/4 CUP LIGHT OLIVE OIL

1. Preheat oven to 325 degrees.
2. Thinly slice the loaf and place the slices in a single layer on a sheet pan.
3. Brush the bread with oil and bake until crisp and golden.

ASSEMBLY: Bear in mind there are three distinct flavor profiles to be offered individually or as a group tasting. When plating, keep the components within a given flavor profile together. Using a vessel or canvas plate large enough to accommodate all of the components is vital to this experience.

A sheet test can be used to determine doneness. Dip a cool metal spoon into the boiling jelly mixture. Lift the spoon 12 inches above the kettle. Let the liquid run off the side of the metal spoon. The jelly is done when 2 big drops slide together and form a sheet that hangs from the edge of the spoon.

**Use baking stencils to achieve various shapes and sizes, which can make everyday recipes special. I prefer to use a spoon-shape mold to make this dish a little more playful.

†"Artisan style" refers to a free-form baked bread, as opposed to a loaf pan-baked bread.

WINE
LATE-HARVEST CHARDONNAY. Picked just before the first frost of the year, the grapes are allowed to mature, giving them concentrated sugars that result in intense fruit flavors of apricot and tropical fruits. The honey aromas and intense mouthfeel are a perfect complement to the peanut butter and the fruit notes of the jam.

BEER
INDIA PALE ALE (IPA). IPAs show robust hop character and bitterness, giving them fantastic floral and citrus notes of orange and grapefruit, and a crisp, dry, and refreshing finish. Founders Brewing Co. Centennial IPA is a perfect example of the style and makes a lovely pairing with this course.

grilled cheese & tomato soup
TOMATILLO CILANTRO BROTH, MANCHEGO CHEESE QUESADILLA, JALAPENO SALT
YELLOW TOMATO CUCUMBER PUREE, AGED WHITE CHEDDAR AND BACON ON SOURDOUGH
ROASTED RED GAZPACHO, FRESH BUFFALO MOZZARELLA ON FOCACCIA, BASIL OIL

LIKE MY RECIPE FOR P, B & J, THIS RECIPE ACTUALLY incorporates three different elements. Combining all three in a trio works great as a plated dish, but each item also works individually as a tapas-style or butler-pass type of dish. It's also worth pointing out that the method for the Jalapeno Salt component can be used to make salts of all different flavors. With this recipe as a starting point, I challenge you to get creative with flavoring salt on your own.

1.

2.

3.

grilled cheese & tomato soup
ROASTED RED GAZPACHO, FRESH BUFFALO MOZZARELLA ON FOCACCIA, BASIL OIL
TOMATILLO CILANTRO BROTH, MANCHEGO CHEESE QUESADILLA, JALAPENO SALT
YELLOW TOMATO CUCUMBER PUREE, AGED WHITE CHEDDAR AND BACON ON SOURDOUGH
SERVES 10

1
TOMATILLO CILANTRO BROTH, MANCHEGO CHEESE QUESADILLA, JALAPENO SALT

TOMATILLO CILANTRO BROTH

2 POUNDS TOMATILLOS, HUSKED, RINSED, AND CORED
1/8 CUP ROUGHLY CHOPPED ONION
1 TABLESPOON LIME ZEST
1 TABLESPOON LIME JUICE
1/2 CUP CHOPPED FRESH CILANTRO
1 JALAPENO, STEMMED, SEEDED, AND CHOPPED
1/4 CUP OLIVE OIL
SEA SALT, TO TASTE

1. In a food processor, puree the tomatillos, onion, and lime zest until they reach a smooth consistency.
2. Add remaining ingredients except olive oil and continue to puree until very smooth.
3. Adjust seasoning and puree in olive oil just before service.

JALAPENO SALT*

2 JALAPENOS, STEMMED AND SEEDED
1/4 CUP KOSHER SALT

1. Preheat oven to 170 degrees.
2. Place peppers and salt in a blender. Puree until smooth and evenly incorporated (about 2 minutes).
3. Spread the mixture thinly over a parchment paper-lined baking sheet.
4. Place in oven and allow to dry for about 1 hour.
5. Once dried, place mixture in a blender and blend until all the crumbles become powder (about 2 minutes). Store in an airtight container.

MANCHEGO CHEESE QUESADILLA

OLIVE OIL, AS NEEDED
3 8-INCH FLOUR TORTILLA SHELLS
1 CUP SHREDDED MANCHEGO CHEESE
JALAPENO SALT (RECIPE ABOVE)

1. Heat a skillet over medium heat.
2. Coat with olive oil and add 1 tortilla.
3. Cover the tortilla with Manchego cheese. When the cheese begins to melt, fold the tortilla in half.
4. Finish cooking the quesadilla until it is golden brown.
5. Season with salt and repeat to make each quesadilla.

2
YELLOW TOMATO CUCUMBER PUREE, AGED WHITE CHEDDAR AND BACON ON SOURDOUGH

YELLOW TOMATO CUCUMBER PUREE

4 LARGE RIPE YELLOW TOMATOES (ABOUT 2 POUNDS), CHOPPED
1 YELLOW BELL PEPPER, CHOPPED
1 SEEDLESS CUCUMBER, CHOPPED
1/4 CUP CHOPPED SHALLOTS
1 TABLESPOON CHOPPED FRESH OREGANO
1/2 CUP OLIVE OIL
1/4 CUP SHERRY VINEGAR
1 CLOVE GARLIC, CHOPPED
SEA SALT, TO TASTE
FRESHLY GROUND WHITE PEPPER, TO TASTE

1. Working in batches as necessary, puree all of the ingredients together in a blender until smooth.
2. Cover and refrigerate for a minimum of 1 hour.
3. Force the soup through a fine-mesh sieve and adjust the flavor to taste with salt and pepper. Whisk before serving.

AGED WHITE CHEDDAR AND BACON ON SOURDOUGH

4 SLICES APPLE WOOD-SMOKED BACON
1 SOURDOUGH LOAF
4 OUNCES BLACK DIAMOND WHITE CHEDDAR**
OLIVE OIL, AS NEEDED

1. Preheat oven to 250 degrees.
2. Lay bacon on a cutting board and slice each piece in half horizontally. Slice each half vertically into thirds. (This should give you a total of six strips out of one piece of bacon.)
3. In a skillet over medium-high heat, render the bacon until crispy. Move to paper towel to drain. Reserve the bacon fat.
4. Slice the sourdough loaf into 1/4-inch-thick pieces.
5. Brush both sides of the bread slices with bacon grease and toast in a skillet over medium heat.
6. Place the sourdough slices on a baking sheet and top them with cheddar slices and rendered bacon.
7. Place in oven to melt the cheddar (about 6 minutes).

3
ROASTED RED GAZPACHO, FRESH BUFFALO MOZZARELLA ON FOCACCIA, BASIL OIL

ROASTED RED GAZPACHO

10 ROMA TOMATOES, CORED
1/2 CUP ROUGHLY CHOPPED RED ONION
3 CLOVES GARLIC, HALVED
1/4 CUP OLIVE OIL
2 TABLESPOONS RED WINE VINEGAR
1/4 CUP PACKED FRESH BASIL
1 CUP TOMATO JUICE
SEA SALT, TO TASTE
FRESHLY CRACKED BLACK PEPPER, TO TASTE

1. Preheat oven to 425 degrees.
2. In a large bowl, mix the tomatoes, onion, garlic, and olive oil.
3. Spread onto a baking sheet and roast in oven until the tomatoes caramelize (about 30 minutes).
4. Allow the mixture to cool and then puree all ingredients, including basil and tomato juice, in a blender until smooth, working in batches as needed.
5. Season with salt and pepper and chill before serving.

BUFFALO MOZZARELLA ON FOCACCIA

1 FOCACCIA LOAF
16 OUNCES BUFFALO MOZZARELLA
KOSHER SALT AND CRACKED BLACK PEPPER, TO TASTE
OLIVE OIL, AS NEEDED
1 TABLESPOON FINELY CHOPPED FRESH BASIL

1. Thinly slice the focaccia bread into 1/4-inch slices.
2. Slice mozzarella into 1/4-inch disks and season to taste with salt and pepper.
3. Heat a skillet over medium heat and coat the bottom with pepper and olive oil.
4. Place focaccia in the hot oil and top it with cheese slices.
5. Sprinkle with the basil and top with a second slice of bread.
6. Drizzle the top with olive oil. Repeat, working in batches of bread and cheese. Flip the sandwiches to brown on both sides, cooking about 3 minutes per side.

ASSEMBLY: These sandwich/soup combinations present terrifically as passed hors d'oeuvres by using a shot glass for the soup and laying the sandwich over the top. For the tasting-style presentation, assemble them the same way, but line them up on a platter-style plate and finish them with the accompanying sandwich, laying it across the top or at the base.

*This ingredient can be easily made or it is commonly found in Latino grocery stores.

**Black Diamond White Cheddar is aged two years for a sharp, robust flavor. If Black Diamond is unavailable, you may substitute another high-quality aged cheddar cheese.

WINE
ROSÉ. In particular, a Spanish rosé, or Rosado, will show lighter red fruits and have a medium acidity that is versatile enough to support heavier flavor profiles yet light enough to not overpower the dish.

BEER
AMERICAN PALE ALE. Amber in color, pale ales are very balanced between bitter hop profiles and caramel-flavored malts. With the delicate balance of flavors in the dish, pairing with a beverage that is neither too light nor too heavy is key. A perfect selection would be Mad Anthony Ol' Woody Pale Ale, produced in Ft. Wayne, Indiana.

mac & goat cheese
PINE NUT-CRUSTED GOAT CHEESE, MACARONI WITH ROASTED RED PEPPER CREAM, SUN-DRIED

I CHOSE TO INCLUDE THIS RECIPE IN THE CHILDHOOD
memories chapter because macaroni & cheese was such a
common meal for so many of us when we were kids. I
started by thinking about the cheese and wondering what
the dish would be like if I put a nice block of really good
goat cheese—along with warm roasted pine nuts—right on
top. Bring in a couple of different supporting cast members
like two pestos and a powder—the result is outstanding.

TOMATO PESTO, BASIL PESTO, CRUSTY OLIVE LOAF

mac & goat cheese
PINE NUT-CRUSTED GOAT CHEESE, MACARONI WITH ROASTED RED PEPPER CREAM, SUN-DRIED TOMATO PESTO
SERVES 10

TOMATO POWDER

10 SUN-DRIED TOMATOES

1. Using a dehydrator, dry the tomatoes at 130 degrees until they are fully crisp.
2. Cool the tomatoes and grind them in a coffee or spice mill into a fine powder.
3. Store in an airtight container.*

SUN-DRIED TOMATO PESTO

6 GARLIC CLOVES
1/4 CUP GRATED PARMESAN CHEESE
1 CUP SUN-DRIED TOMATOES
1 TABLESPOON BALSAMIC SYRUP**
1/4 CUP PINE NUTS
1/2 CUP OLIVE OIL
2 TABLESPOONS FINELY CHOPPED OREGANO
KOSHER SALT, TO TASTE
GROUND BLACK PEPPER, TO TASTE

1. In a food processor, pulse the garlic, cheese, tomatoes, balsamic syrup, and pine nuts.
2. With the motor running, add the oil and blend until the ingredients are incorporated.
3. Fold in the chopped oregano and season to taste with salt and pepper.

BASIL PESTO

YIELDS ABOUT 2 1/2 CUPS

2 GARLIC CLOVES
1/4 CUP PINE NUTS
1/2 CUP GRATED PARMIGIANO-REGGIANO CHEESE
1 CUP PACKED BASIL LEAVES
1/2 CUP LOOSELY PACKED FRESH LEMON BASIL LEAVES
1/2 CUP PACKED FLAT-LEAF PARSLEY LEAVES
1/2 TEASPOON GROUND BLACK PEPPER, OR AS NEEDED
1/3 CUP OLIVE OIL
SEA SALT, TO TASTE

1. In a food processor, pulse the garlic until it is finely chopped.
2. Add the pine nuts, Parmigiano-Reggiano, a large handful of the herbs, and 1/2 teaspoon pepper, and process until chopped.
3. Add the remaining herbs to the food processor and pulse until they are finely chopped.
4. With the motor running, add the oil and blend until the ingredients are incorporated. Season to taste with sea salt. Store pesto in refrigerator for up to 2 weeks.

GOAT CHEESE MACARONI

1 POUND MACARONI
VEGETABLE OIL, AS NEEDED
1 TABLESPOON BUTTER
2 GARLIC CLOVES, FINELY CHOPPED
1 CUP WHITE WINE
2 CUPS HEAVY CREAM
1 CUP GOAT CHEESE (8 OUNCES)
SEA SALT, TO TASTE
FINELY GROUND WHITE PEPPER, TO TASTE

1. Cook the macaroni in boiling salted water until it is al dente (just cooked).
2. Shock the pasta in cold water, drain it well, oil it lightly, and then reserve.
3. Melt the butter in a medium-size saucepan over medium-low heat. Sweat the garlic and then add the white wine and cream. Simmer for 5 minutes and reduce the liquid by half.
4. Whisk in the goat cheese and continue to simmer the mixture until it has reached a nappe consistency. Season to taste with salt and pepper.†
5. Just before serving, blend the macaroni into the warm sauce and simmer until it is hot, stirring occasionally to thoroughly incorporate the sauce.

ROASTED RED BELL PEPPER CREAM SAUCE

YIELDS ABOUT 1 CUP

3 LARGE RED BELL PEPPERS
1/2 CUP WHITE WINE
1 TABLESPOON CHOPPED GARLIC
2 CUPS HEAVY WHIPPING CREAM
1/2 CUP GRATED PARMESAN CHEESE
KOSHER SALT, TO TASTE
FRESHLY GROUND WHITE PEPPER, TO TASTE

1. Char the peppers over a flame or under a broiler until they are blackened on all sides. Enclose them in a paper bag and let them stand for 10 minutes.
2. Peel, seed, and coarsely chop the peppers.
3. Transfer them to a saucepan over medium heat and add the wine and garlic; reduce the liquid by half.
4. Add the cream and reduce by half again.
5. Using a stick blender, puree the mixture until smooth. (You may also transfer the mixture to a food processor and puree, returning the mixture to the pan when it is smooth.)
6. Add the Parmesan cheese, stirring to melt it completely.
7. Season to taste with salt and pepper. Stir the sauce well before service.

WINE
SANCERRE. A traditional pairing of the Loire Valley region in France (where the grapes originate), Sancerre and goat cheese are perfect together. Made from Sauvignon Blanc grapes, it carries mineral notes of flint and gravel, and is crisp and snappy on the palate, lifting out the creamy texture of the goat cheese beautifully.

BEER
BELGIAN TRIPEL. Pale gold in color, the Tripel is a full-bodied ale that carries great fruity and spicy notes with a dry and spirituous finish that will both compliment and contrast the goat cheese, pine nuts, and pesto components of the dish.

PINE NUT-CRUSTED GOAT CHEESE

16 OUNCES FRESH GOAT CHEESE (LOG SHAPE)
KOSHER SALT, TO TASTE
CRACKED BLACK PEPPER, TO TASTE
1 CUP PINE NUTS, CHOPPED

1. Using a hot, clean knife, portion the goat cheese into 1$\frac{1}{2}$-ounce medallions (about $\frac{3}{4}$ inch thick).
2. Season to taste with salt and pepper.
3. Toast the pine nuts in a small skillet over medium heat. Be careful not to burn them. While the pine nuts are still hot, press one side of the cheese medallions into the nuts to set a nice crust. These need to be served immediately.

ASSEMBLY: Use a vessel that allows plenty of space for laying out the components of this dish, while keeping the pasta feel in mind. Your favorite crusty bread can be used. Olive loaf is a great choice to accentuate the pesto varieties. Portion the creamy goat cheese macaroni in the center of the vessel. Spoon some roasted red pepper sauce along the edge of the pasta. Portion some of the tomato pesto and basil pesto on top of the pasta, keeping them separate. Top the pasta with a pine nut-crusted medallion of goat cheese. Sprinkle the dish with tomato powder. Serve with slices of crusty bread.

*Tomato powder is a gateway to a world of dusts. Creativity will drive cooks to use this ingredient in many different applications. If you are looking for a tomato flavor without pieces of tomato in the dish, this would be a perfect substitute.

**To make balsamic syrup, place $\frac{1}{4}$ cup balsamic vinegar in a small saucepan over medium heat and reduce until it has reached a syrupy consistency. Use any extra balsamic syrup to drizzle over pieces of toasted bread with good cheese or over salad greens.

†"Nappe" refers to the ability of a liquid to coat the back of a spoon.

fish & chips (two ways)

CRISPY CORNMEAL-CRUSTED WALLEYE, CHIVE POLENTA CAKE,
  ROASTED CORN TARTAR SAUCE, MALT VINEGAR REDUCTION, FRIED POTATO NET
HERB-GRILLED HALIBUT, CHIVE POLENTA CAKE, FRIED POTATO NET,
  MALT VINEGAR BEURRE BLANC

SERVES 10

THERE ARE TWO DIFFERENT VERSIONS OF THIS DISH, ONE OF
  which takes me to the shores of Lake of the Woods in
  Canada, fishing for walleye. The local guides fix this fresh
  walleye right on the shore. The second version is for a
  fired-up summer grill and a great herb-marinated piece of
  halibut. The fish takes on the smokiness of open flame as
  the oils char to varying degrees. (Of course, the degree of
  charring depends on who is cooking.)

1

**CRISPY CORNMEAL-CRUSTED WALLEYE, CHIVE POLENTA
CAKE, ROASTED CORN TARTER SAUCE, MALT VINEGAR
REDUCTION, FRIED POTATO NET**

CRISPY CORNMEAL-CRUSTED WALLEYE

    CANOLA OIL, FOR DEEP-FRYING
    3 POUNDS BONELESS WALLEYE FILETS,
        CUT INTO 4- OR 5-INCH PIECES

EGG WASH

    4 LARGE EGGS
    1/2 CUP WATER

SEASONED FLOUR

    2 CUPS ALL-PURPOSE FLOUR
    1 TEASPOON KOSHER SALT
    1/2 TEASPOON GROUND BLACK PEPPER

CORNMEAL BREADING

    1 CUP CORNMEAL
    1/2 CUP OYSTER CRACKERS
    1/2 TEASPOON OLD BAY SEASONING
    1/2 TEASPOON SEA SALT
    1/2 TEASPOON GROUND BLACK PEPPER
    1/2 TEASPOON GRANULATED GARLIC
    1 TEASPOON DRIED PARSLEY

1. Start by heating the oil to 350 degrees in a deep-sided frying pan.
2. While the oil is coming to temperature, whisk together the
eggs and water until a smooth egg wash is made.
3. In a separate bowl, combine the seasoned flour ingredients.
4. Place all of the cornmeal breading ingredients in a food
processor and puree until it is a well-incorporated powder.
5. Place the walleye in the seasoned flour and coat well.
6. Shake off the excess flour and place the fish in the egg
wash for a few minutes.
7. Transfer to the cornmeal mixture and coat.
8. Fry the fish in oil, turning it as needed, until just cooked (120
degree internal temperature).

ROASTED CORN TARTAR SAUCE

    3 EARS CORN, HUSKED
    1 CUP MAYONNAISE
    1/4 CUP FINELY CHOPPED DILL PICKLES
    3 TABLESPOONS CHOPPED GREEN ONIONS
    1 TABLESPOON DRAINED CAPERS
    1 TABLESPOON CHOPPED FRESH PARLEY
    2 TEASPOONS LEMON JUICE
    1 TEASPOON DIJON MUSTARD
    1/2 TEASPOON WORCESTERSHIRE SAUCE
    1/4 TEASPOON HOT PEPPER SAUCE
    KOSHER SALT, TO TASTE
    GROUND BLACK PEPPER, TO TASTE

1. Prepare an ice water bath.
2. Blanch the corn in boiling water until it is just tender and
then place the ears in ice water.
3. Preheat grill or large saute pan and over medium-high heat
and roast the corn until it is caramelized.
4. Remove the corn kernels from the ears.
5. Whisk all of the tartar sauce ingredients in a medium-sized
bowl to blend.
6. Season to taste with salt and pepper, cover, and chill at least
1 hour or up to 2 days before serving.

MALT VINEGAR REDUCTION

    1 CUP MALT VINEGAR
    2 TABLESPOONS GRANULATED SUGAR

1. Pour vinegar into a stainless steel sauce pan.
2. Over medium heat, reduce vinegar by 1/2 the volume.
3. Add sugar and continue to simmer for 5 minutes.
4. Remove from heat and serve at room temperature. (This can
be made up to 2 days before serving).

1.

fish & chips

CRISPY CORNMEAL-CRUSTED WALLEYE, CHIVE POLENTA CAKE, ROASTED CORN TARTAR SAUCE,
MALT VINEGAR REDUCTION, FRIED POTATO NET
HERB-GRILLED HALIBUT, CHIVE POLENTA CAKE, FRIED POTATO NET, MALT VINEGAR BEURRE BLANC

2
HERB-GRILLED HALIBUT, CHIVE POLENTA CAKE, FRIED POTATO NET, MALT VINEGAR BEURRE BLANC

HERB-GRILLED HALIBUT

1 TABLESPOON CHOPPED FRESH THYME
1 TABLESPOON CHOPPED FRESH OREGANO
1 TABLESPOON CHOPPED FRESH CHIVES
2 TABLESPOONS OLIVE OIL
1/4 CUP WHITE WINE
1 TEASPOON SEA SALT
1/2 TEASPOON GROUND BLACK PEPPER
8 5-OUNCE HALIBUT FILETS

1. Combine all of the ingredients except the halibut in a non-corrosive pan. Marinate the fish in this marinade for 20 minutes before grilling.
2. Grill fish over medium-high heat until it reaches 120 degrees internal temperature.

MALT VINEGAR BEURRE BLANC

1/2 CUP DRY WHITE WINE
2 TABLESPOONS ROUGHLY CHOPPED SHALLOT
2 TABLESPOONS MALT VINEGAR
1/4 CUP HEAVY CREAM
1 CUP UNSALTED BUTTER, CUT INTO TABLESPOON-SIZED
  PIECES AND CHILLED
SEA SALT, TO TASTE
FRESHLY GROUND WHITE PEPPER, TO TASTE

1. Boil the wine, shallot, and vinegar in a heavy medium-sized saucepan over medium-high heat until the liquid is reduced to about 2 tablespoons (about 5 minutes).
2. Add the cream and bring to a boil for about 1 minute.
3. Reduce heat to low and add a few pieces of the butter, whisking constantly. Once the butter has melted and is incorporated, add the remaining tablespoons of butter a few pieces at a time. Remove the pan from the heat occasionally, if needed, to cool mixture. (If the mixture gets too hot, the butter will separate from the reduction, and you will end up with an un-emulsified sauce.)
4. Once all of the butter is incorporated, remove the sauce from heat and season to taste with salt and pepper.
5. Pass the sauce through a fine-mesh sieve at least once and discard the shallot. The sauce should be velvety and smooth.
6. Adjust the flavor with additional malt vinegar, if desired.

ACCOMPANIMENTS

CHIVE POLENTA CAKE

3 CUPS CHICKEN STOCK
1 CUP POLENTA (CORNMEAL)
1/2 CUP HEAVY WHIPPING CREAM
1/4 CUP CHOPPED FRESH CHIVES
KOSHER SALT, TO TASTE
FRESHLY GROUND WHITE PEPPER, TO TASTE
OLIVE OIL, AS NEEDED

1. Place the cold stock and polenta in a heavy saucepan and bring to a simmer over medium heat, stirring frequently. Simmer the polenta until it is tender and the mixture thickens (about 20 minutes).
2. Stir in cream and cook for 3 minutes. Remove from heat.
3. Stir in chives and adjust flavor to taste with salt and pepper.
4. While the polenta is hot, pour it into a plastic-lined 9-inch baking pan and chill in refrigerator.
5. Once it is cool, remove the polenta cake by lifting out the plastic lining. Cut it into desired portions (about 12-16 squares).
6. In a nonstick skillet over medium heat with olive oil, toast the polenta cake on both sides. Serve immediately or keep warm in the oven until service.

FRIED POTATO NET *

4 RUSSET POTATOES (ABOUT 2 POUNDS)
ABOUT 4 CUPS CANOLA OIL, FOR DEEP-FRYING

1. Peel the potatoes and put them in a bowl of cold water so they are submerged.
2. Remove 1 potato and pat dry.
3. Using a mandoline or another manual slicer, cut the potato into paper-thin slices (about 1/16 inch thick) and let the potato slices stand 5 minutes in another bowl of cold water to cover.
4. In a 3-quart saucepan, heat the oil until a deep-fat thermometer registers 350 degrees Fahrenheit.
5. While the oil is coming to temperature, finish preparing the sliced potatoes. You will need a rolling net cutter and mat to create the lacy patterns for the potatoes. **

6. Dry 1 potato slice with paper towel and place it on the mat. Roll the cutter over the potato, leaving 1 end intact.

7. Transfer the net to the oil, using a pair of tongs to keep the net open during frying. Fry until golden (about 1 minute).

8. Repeat for each potato net, making sure the oil returns to 350 degrees before adding a potato.

9. As they are fried, use a large slotted spoon to transfer the potatoes to paper towels to drain and then sprinkle with salt. Repeat for each net. The potato nets may be made a few hours ahead and kept in an airtight container.

*Gaufrette chips can also be used with this dish. See recipe on page 113.

**A "rolling net cutter" is used to create a net pattern out of vegetables that have been thinly sliced. It can be purchased from JB Prince (jbprince.com) or another chef's tool supplier.

2.

french toast & orange juice

GRAND MARNIER-SCENTED FRENCH TOAST, POMEGRANATE SYRUP, MANGO CHUTNEY, BLOOD

SERVES 12

A FAVORITE CHILDHOOD BREAKFAST-TURNED-DESSERT, this dish is absolutely delicious at a late-night affair with friends. It's a terrific way to end a long evening that may have crept its way into the early morning hours.

GRAND MARNIER-SCENTED FRENCH TOAST

ORANGE POUND CAKE*

SERVES 12

1 1/4 CUPS UNSALTED BUTTER, ROOM TEMPERATURE, PLUS MORE TO PREPARE PAN
1 3/4 CUPS GRANULATED SUGAR
6 LARGE EGGS
2 TABLESPOONS ORANGE JUICE
2 TABLESPOONS ORANGE ZEST
1 TABLESPOON VANILLA EXTRACT
2 CUPS ALL-PURPOSE FLOUR, PLUS MORE TO PREPARE PAN
1/2 TEASPOON KOSHER SALT

1. Preheat oven to 325 degrees.
2. Butter and flour a 12-cup loaf pan.
3. Using an electric mixer, beat 1 1/4 cups butter in a large bowl until smooth.
4. Gradually add the sugar, beating the mixture until it is fluffy.
5. Beat in the eggs 1 at a time.
6. Beat in the orange juice, orange zest, and vanilla.
7. Add the flour and salt and then beat just until blended.
8. Transfer the batter to the prepared pan.
9. Bake the cake in the oven until golden and a tester such as a toothpick inserted near the center comes out clean (about 1 hour, 5 minutes).
10. Cool the cake in the pan on a rack for 10 minutes.
11. Invert the cake onto the rack to cool completely. (This can be made 1 day ahead of serving. Wrap it in plastic and then store at room temperature.)

POMEGRANATE SYRUP*

2 CUPS POMEGRANATE JUICE
1 1/2 CUPS SUGAR
1 TEASPOON LEMON JUICE

1. In a saucepan over medium heat, combine the pomegranate juice, sugar, and lemon juice.
2. Stir until the sugar has completely dissolved. Allow the mixture to simmer over medium heat until the juice is the consistency of syrup (about 20-25 minutes).
3. Remove the pan from heat and allow the syrup to cool. Store in an airtight container in the refrigerator for up to 2 weeks.

MANGO CHUTNEY*

3 MANGOS
1/2 CUP SUGAR
1 CUP WATER
3 CINNAMON STICKS
1 CUP MANGO NECTAR**

1. Peel the mangos and cut the meat off of the seed. (The seed is shaped like a used-up bar of soap; stand the mango on its base and slice down along the sides of the seed.)
2. Brunoise the tender mango meat, cutting it first into 1/8-inch matchsticks and then into 1/8-inch cubes. Set aside.†
3. Place the peelings and pits in a heavy saucepan.
4. Add the sugar, water, cinnamon, and nectar. Bring to a boil.
5. Reduce heat and simmer until syrup is formed.
6. Strain the mixture through a fine-mesh sieve and then allow it to cool.
7. Stir in the mango meat and store in an airtight container in the refrigerator for up to 4 days.

FRENCH TOAST

SERVES 12

5 LARGE EGGS
3/4 CUP HALF-AND-HALF
2 TABLESPOONS GRAND MARNIER OR OTHER ORANGE-FLAVORED LIQUEUR
3 TABLESPOONS POWDERED SUGAR
2 TEASPOONS ORANGE ZEST
1/2 TEASPOON VANILLA EXTRACT
4 TABLESPOONS (1/2 STICK) BUTTER

1. Cut the Orange Pound Cake into 12 equal slices.
2. In a medium-sized mixing bowl, whisk together the first 6 ingredients (everything except butter) to blend well.
3. Melt the butter in a skillet over medium heat.
4. Dip each cake slice into the batter quickly and panfry on both sides until golden brown. (Do not soak the pound cake in the batter.)

ORANGE JULIUS

1 6-OUNCE CAN FROZEN CONCENTRATE ORANGE JUICE
1 CUP MILK
2 CUPS VANILLA ICE CREAM
1 TABLESPOON BLOOD ORANGE ZEST

1. Put all of the ingredients in a blender.
2. Blend about 30 seconds.
3. Serve immediately or keep in freezer if necessary. (It may have to be thawed and re-blended, depending on how long it is in the freezer before service.)

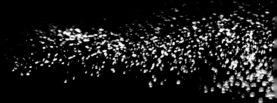

ORANGE JULIUS

BLOOD ORANGE SYRUP*

YIELDS 1 ½ CUPS

3 CUPS FRESH BLOOD ORANGE JUICE
9 TABLESPOONS GRANULATED SUGAR

1. Place the juice and sugar in a heavy medium-size saucepan over medium heat until the sugar dissolves.
2. Increase the heat and boil until the syrup is reduced to 1½ cups (about 20 minutes).
3. Refrigerate until it is cold.

ASSEMBLY: This dish presents itself nicely as the items are served next to each other. If your plate has enough space, you can incorporate the orange julius into the presentation as a small shooter.

Cut each French toast slice corner to corner, so that you get two triangles. Serve the French toast as a stack or shingle the slices, topping it with the mango chutney and drizzling it with the pomegranate syrup. Finish the stack off by dusting it with powdered sugar. Drizzle some orange syrup into the bottom of a frozen glass before filling the rest of the way with the Julius.

*These recipes can be easily made the day prior to assemby.

**Mango nectar is made from mango juice and pulp and is sometimes labeled "mango juice."

†A "brunoise" cut refers to cutting the ingredient first into ⅛-inch matchsticks and then into ⅛-inch cubes.

WINE
MUSCAT (ORANGE). Sweet, yet still crisp on the palate, wines made from the orange variety of the Muscat grape show bright notes of apricot, ripe peach, honey and, of course, orange. Quady Electra is an easily obtainable label that would work great for this pairing.

BEER
AMERICAN WHEAT. Typically hazy yellow to orange in color and very light-bodied, these beers show a spritzy, citric, and slightly tangy mouthfeel with a subtle spice presence that is clean and refreshing between bites. Left Hand Haystack Wheat from Colorado is a perfect choice for the dish.

brownie & milk

RUM FUDGE BROWNIE, DRUNKEN EGGNOG MILKSHAKE

SERVES 12

THIS IS A VERY BASIC CONCEPT, PERHAPS REMINISCENT of a late-night snack you might leave out for Saint Nick on Christmas Eve. At the same time, it is so much more than just a brownie and milk.

RUM FUDGE BROWNIE

YIELDS 1 9-INCH PAN

1 POUND DARK CHOCOLATE
1 POUND (4 STICKS) UNSALTED BUTTER, CUBED
4 EGGS
1 3/4 CUPS GRANULATED SUGAR
1 1/8 CUPS ALL-PURPOSE FLOUR
1 PINCH KOSHER SALT
1 TEASPOON VANILLA EXTRACT
3/4 CUP 10 CANE RUM

1. Preheat oven to 325 degrees.
2. Gently melt the chocolate in a double boiler over medium-low heat.
3. Once completely melted, turn heat to low and add the butter, stirring constantly. Be careful not to allow butter to break. Once it is incorporated, remove from heat.
4. In a mixing bowl, whisk together the eggs and sugar.
5. Add the flour and continue whisking until smooth.
6. Add the salt, vanilla, and rum.
7. Finally, incorporate the chocolate mixture into the batter.
8. Pour the chocolate batter into a greased 9-inch baking pan. Cover the pan with plastic and then foil, being sure to get a good seal.
9. Bake in a shallow water bath until the mixture reaches 135 degrees internal temperature.
10. Remove pan from the oven and water bath, uncover it, and chill in the refrigerator. The brownie will set when cold. Serve chilled. Prior to plating, cut brownie using a heated knife, wiping blade between cuts.

DRUNKEN EGGNOG MILKSHAKE

MAKES ABOUT 1 1/2 QUARTS

1/2 CUP WHOLE MILK
1/8 TEASPOON SALT
4 LARGE EGG YOLKS
1/2 CUP GRANULATED SUGAR
1 CUP CHILLED HEAVY CREAM
3 TABLESPOONS DARK RUM
1/4 TEASPOON FRESHLY GRATED NUTMEG
2 1/2 CUPS HIGH-QUALITY VANILLA BEAN ICE CREAM

1. Bring the milk and salt to a low simmer in a heavy saucepan.
2. In a mixing bowl, whisk together the egg yolks and sugar.
3. Gradually add the hot milk to the yolk mixture, whisking continually to prevent the eggs from curdling.
4. Return the mixture to the heavy saucepan and cook the custard over low heat, stirring constantly until the mixture is thickened and coats the back of a spoon.
5. Immediately pour the mixture through a fine-mesh sieve into a large clean bowl.
6. Add the cream, rum, and nutmeg.
7. Chill the prepared custard in the refrigerator until it is cold (about 2 hours).
8. Put the custard and vanilla bean ice cream in a blender and mix until smooth. (Additional rum can be added and consistency can be adjusted with milk, if needed.) Serve immediately in a tall, frozen glass.

ASSEMBLY: Serve the milkshake in frozen glasses. Serve the brownies in small portions, due to their excessive richness. Garnish the top of each milkshake with freshly ground nutmeg.

SPIRIT
GOLDEN RUM. I much prefer good rum or beer (see suggestion below) rather than wine in this instance. Golden rum, without spices and served chilled, will pull out the notes of the rum-infused characters in the eggnog and the brownie.

BEER
IMPERIAL STOUT. These dark, rich beers carry natural notes of chocolate, toasted nuts, and coffee from their roasted malts and have a smooth and silky finish. The ultimate pairing choices would be oak-aged or bourbon barrel-aged stouts, preferably Great Divide's Oak Aged Yeti Imperial Stout from Colorado.

compare
and contrast

THE PREMISE OF THIS CHAPTER IS, QUITE SIMPLY, TO PIT DIFFERENT KINDS OF FOODS AND PREPARATIONS AGAINST EACH OTHER. IT'S A GOOD WAY TO EXERCISE YOUR PALATE.

COOKING AND EATING IN THIS WAY RAISES IMPORTANT questions: What do you find different about the preparations you've made? How are they the same? Which do you like best? I designed the "Compare & Contrast" concept to help people get down to the nitty-gritty of their own palates by exploring how a wide range of preparations can affect the flavor and texture of a single ingredient, or how using similar-but-different ingredients can affect the final outcome of a dish.

Another intention of this chapter is to encourage you to get to know your own palate, and to think about even the simplest of ingredients in new ways. Americans in particular tend to think that whichever ingredient is most expensive must also be the best. If that's how you feel, I'd like to show you that cost is not the most important factor

in how special an ingredient is. The more important driver is what can be done with it. Lobster is expensive, but it lends itself to only a relatively small number of applications. A pear, on the other hand, is something you can often get free from a tree in someone's back yard, and it's amazing what you can do with it. In my recipes "A Taste of Pear", the fruit is cooked to a soft consistency in a cobbler, pureed into butter, frozen as ice cream, and oven-dried into chips. All I've done is put pear dishes in front of you. Trying pear in so many different variations pushes your palate to appreciate it in all of its simplicity.

"cost is not the most important factor in how special an ingredient is. the more important driver is what can be done with it."

trio of crab

LAZY MAN'S KING CRAB LEGS, LIME VINAIGRETTE; CRAB AVOCADO SALAD, MICRO CILANTRO

THE LAZY MAN'S KING CRAB LEGS ARE INTENDED TO SHOW
that there is almost nothing better than eating crab legs
when you don't have to crack the shell and pull the meat
out on your own. When you use the "lazy man" style, the
work is done on the front end, so when it's time to sit down
and eat, all you have to do is enjoy, rather than cracking the
crab and slopping it everywhere. It's a nice way to reward
your diners. The procedure also allows you to influence the
crab with butter while you're warming it, as opposed to
just bringing it up with steam then dipping it in butter at
the table.

trio of crab

LAZY MAN'S KING CRAB LEGS, LIME VINAIGRETTE
CRAB AVOCADO SALAD, MICRO CILANTRO, MANGO GINGER SHOOTER
JUMBO LUMP CRAB CAKE, CARAMELIZED PINEAPPLE, JALAPENO AIOLI

SERVES 10

LAZY MAN'S KING CRAB LEGS, LIME VINAIGRETTE

LAZY MAN'S KING CRAB LEGS

10 LARGE KING CRAB LEGS
1/4 CUP UNSALTED BUTTER, MELTED
1 CUP WHITE WINE

1. Preheat oven to 300 degrees.
2. Using kitchen shears, cut each of the legs in half at the joint. Gently split the legs lengthwise on both sides, resulting in 2 sections of shell for each leg section. Gently remove the meat and then reposition it onto 1 piece of the shell. Discard the other shells.
3. Position all of the exposed crabmeat on the shells into a shallow baking pan and brush generously with melted butter.
4. Pour white wine into the bottom of the pan underneath the crab legs.
5. Cover and seal the pan with foil and then warm the crab legs in the oven (approximately 10 minutes).

LIME VINAIGRETTE

1 EGG YOLK
1 TEASPOON DIJON MUSTARD
1/4 CUP CHAMPAGNE VINEGAR
1/4 CUP LIME JUICE
1/8 CUP SUGAR
1 TEASPOON LIME ZEST
1 CUP CANOLA OIL
KOSHER SALT, TO TASTE
GROUND WHITE PEPPER, TO TASTE

1. Using a stick blender or a whisk, mix the first 6 ingredients (egg yolk, mustard, vinegar, lime juice, sugar, and lime zest) until smooth.
2. While continuing to blend, slowly stream in the oil.
3. Season to taste with salt and pepper.

CRAB AVOCADO SALAD, MICRO CILANTRO, MANGO GINGER SHOOTER

CRAB AVOCADO SALAD

2 TABLESPOONS FINELY CHOPPED RED ONION
3 TABLESPOONS OLIVE OIL
2 TABLESPOONS CHAMPAGNE VINEGAR
2 TABLESPOONS FINELY CHOPPED FRESH CILANTRO
3 TEASPOONS FRESH LIME JUICE
1/2 TEASPOON GROUND CUMIN
1/2 TEASPOON GRATED LIME ZEST
8 OUNCES JUMBO LUMP CRABMEAT
SEA SALT, TO TASTE
GROUND BLACK PEPPER, TO TASTE
1 LARGE RIPE AVOCADO, HALVED, PITTED, AND PEELED

1. Stir the red onion, olive oil, champagne vinegar, cilantro, 2 teaspoons of the lime juice, cumin, and lime zest together in a medium-size bowl to blend.
2. Gently mix in the crabmeat.
3. Season the salad to taste with salt and pepper.
4. Slice the avocado into thin slices and brush with the remaining 1 teaspoon lime juice to prevent discoloration. Season to taste with sea salt and pepper.

MANGO GINGER SHOOTER

1 CUP MANGO NECTAR*
1 CUP WATER
2 TABLESPOONS GRANULATED SUGAR
1/2 CUP PEELED, THINLY SLICED FRESH GINGER
2 TABLESPOONS LEMON JUICE
1 CUP PEELED, CHOPPED FRESH MANGO

1. Combine all ingredients in a heavy saucepan and gently simmer for 30 minutes.
2. Chill in the refrigerator and then strain. Serve cold.

JUMBO LUMP CRAB CAKE, CARAMELIZED PINEAPPLE, JALAPENO AIOLI

JUMBO LUMP CRAB CAKE

1/2 CUP FINELY CHOPPED RED ONION
1/4 CUP UNSALTED BUTTER
1/2 CUP WHITE WINE
1 POUND JUMBO LUMP CRABMEAT, PICKED OVER
A FEW DASHES TABASCO
2 TABLESPOONS MINCED FRESH FLAT-LEAF PARSLEY LEAVES
2 TABLESPOONS LEMON JUICE
1/3 CUP FINE DRY BREAD CRUMBS
1 EGG
SEA SALT, TO TASTE
GROUND BLACK PEPPER, TO TASTE
2 TABLESPOONS OLIVE OIL, AS NEEDED

1. In a skillet, cook the onion in 2 tablespoons of the butter over moderately low heat, stirring until it is tender.
2. Deglaze the pan with wine and reduce the liquid by half. Remove from heat and whisk in the remaining 6 tablespoons of butter to form a beurre blanc. Set aside.**
3. In a separate bowl, combine the crabmeat, Tabasco, parsley, lemon juice, bread crumbs, and egg.
4. Gently fold in the onion butter mixture and adjust the seasoning to taste with salt and pepper.
5. Form the crab cakes approximately 1 1/2 inches in diameter and 3/4-inch thickness.
6. Chill the crab cakes, covered with plastic wrap, for at least 1 hour and up to 4 hours before cooking.
7. In a heavy skillet, heat the olive oil over moderate heat and cook the crab cakes until they are golden brown (about 2 minutes on each side).

JALAPENO AIOLI

1 CUP MAYONNAISE
1 TABLESPOON FINELY CHOPPED CHIVES
2 MINCED GARLIC CLOVES
2 TEASPOONS FRESH LIME JUICE
2 TABLESPOONS MINCED JALAPENO (SEEDS DISCARDED)
KOSHER SALT, TO TASTE
GROUND WHITE PEPPER, TO TASTE

1. Whisk together the mayonnaise, chives, garlic, lime juice, and jalapeno.
2. Season to taste with salt and pepper and chill until service.

CARAMELIZED PINEAPPLE

10 PINEAPPLE SLICES (NO SKIN, NO CORE, APPROXIMATELY 2 INCHES SQUARE AND 1/4 INCH THICK)
1 TABLESPOON TURBINADO SUGAR

1. Sprinkle the pineapple slices with a small amount of sugar.
2. Use a kitchen torch to caramelize the pineapple. Keep the torch moving to prevent burning the pineapple and to achieve even caramelization.

ASSEMBLY: This dish has a terrific balance of offerings. You have cold, hot and warm from a temperature aspect, and from a spice (heat) aspect, you have refreshing (Mango Ginger Shooter) and sweet (crab legs) to plenty of spice in the aioli. The Lime Vinaigrette is your liaison amongst the three items. Working with plenty of plate space, top the Caramelized Pineapple with the crab cake and finish that with the aioli. Next, position the Lazy Man's King Crab Legs, dripping with a healthy amount of the Lime Vinaigrette. Finally, the Mango Ginger Shooter accompanies the Crab Avocado Salad. Keep everything tight and flowing. Also, the crab legs make an excellent dividing component for the other two.

*Mango nectar is made from mango juice and pulp and is sometimes labeled "mango juice."

**Meaning "white butter," this classic French sauce is composed of a wine reduction into which chunks of cold butter are whisked until the sauce is thick and smooth.

WINE
SAUVIGNON BLANC. A preferable variety is one from New Zealand, with bright notes of lemongrass, lime, and grapefruit on the nose, and a crisp and refreshing palate that finishes tart and very dry. Cloudy Bay Sauvignon Blanc from the Marlborough Valley is an excellent match.

BEER
BELGIAN SAISON. The most versatile beer for most food pairings, saison, or farmhouse-style ales, are very approachable, with slight grassy and citrus notes on the nose, and a snappy, racy mouthfeel that finishes very dry. The crisp finish and high carbonation make it a fantastic match for nearly all shellfish and spicy dishes. Saison Dupont is the absolute classic example of the style.

lobster soup & salad

BUTTER-POACHED LOBSTER CLAW, LOBSTER FENNEL BISQUE
GRILLED LOBSTER TAIL, FRISÉE AND RADISH SALAD, CHAMPAGNE LEMON VINAIGRETTE,
DILL OIL

THIS IS A SIMPLE CONCEPT, BUT ONE THAT NEEDS TO BE
executed well to reach its full potential. Lobster is very
delicate; if it is treated with respect, the reward will be true.
There may be a bit of an intimidation factor in approaching
this dish, but some of the components, such as the Lobster
Fennel Bisque and the Dill Oil, can be made ahead of time
to make the preparation easier. Then you can concentrate
on poaching the claw and grilling the tail perfectly.

lobster soup & salad

BUTTER-POACHED LOBSTER CLAW, LOBSTER FENNEL BISQUE
GRILLED LOBSTER TAIL, FRISÉE AND RADISH SALAD, CHAMPAGNE LEMON VINAIGRETTE, DILL OIL
SERVES 8

LOBSTER FENNEL BISQUE

4 1 1/2-POUND LIVE LOBSTERS
2 TABLESPOONS UNSALTED BUTTER
1 ONION, SLICED
2 BULBS FENNEL, SLICED
1 LARGE CELERY STALK, SLICED
1 GARLIC HEAD, CUT IN HALF CROSSWISE
3 SPRIGS THYME
2 BAY LEAVES
8 WHOLE BLACK PEPPERCORNS
1 CUP WHITE WINE
4 CUPS LOBSTER STOCK OR SEAFOOD STOCK
1 CUP HEAVY WHIPPING CREAM
2 TEASPOONS CORNSTARCH
1 TABLESPOON WATER

1. Prepare a large bowl of ice water and set aside.
2. Bring a large pot of water to a boil.
3. Add the lobsters and boil for 2-3 minutes. Be sure that the water returns to a boil quickly; you may need to cook them 1 at a time.
4. Using tongs, transfer the lobsters to the bowl of ice water and allow them to cool.
5. Working over a large bowl or pan to catch the juices, cut off the lobster tails and claws. Split the tails gently with shears and remove the meat. Using the back of a heavy knife or shears, crack the claws and gently remove the meat in 1 piece. All of the claw meat and tail meat should still be raw and should be covered and refrigerated for later.
6. Coarsely chop the lobster shells and bodies; reserve juices from lobster in the large bowl.
7. Heat the butter in large, heavy pot over medium-high heat.
8. Add the lobster shells and bodies and saute until the shells begin to brown (about 8 minutes).
9. Add the onion, fennel, celery, garlic, thyme, bay leaves, and peppercorns. Continue sauteing for 5 minutes and then add the wine. Simmer until almost all of the liquid has evaporated (about 10 minutes).
10. Add the stock and reserved lobster juices. Gently simmer this for 1 hour.
11. Strain the soup through a sieve set over a large saucepan, pressing firmly on solids; discard the solids.
12. Continue simmering the broth until it is reduced to 3-4 cups (about 15 minutes).
13. Temper the cream into the soup (adding it gradually while stirring briskly) and simmer for 5 minutes.
14. In a small bowl, dissolve the cornstarch into the 1 tablespoon water. Add this to the soup and boil until slightly thickened (about 3 minutes). Keep warm for service.

BUTTER-POACHED LOBSTER CLAWS

1/2 CUP WHITE WINE
8 LOBSTER CLAWS (MEAT REMOVED)
1/2 CUP UNSALTED BUTTER, CUBED
SEA SALT, TO TASTE

1. In a saute pan, bring the white wine to a simmer.
2. Add the lobster claw meat and reduce the wine by half (about 3 minutes).
3. Reduce the heat to low and melt in the butter.
4. Season to taste with sea salt and continue gently poaching the lobster claw meat in the beurre blanc for a few minutes until just done. Serve immediately.*

GRILLED LOBSTER TAIL

4 SHELLED COLD-WATER LOBSTER TAILS,
   SLICED INTO MEDALLIONS
1 TABLESPOON LEMON JUICE
1/2 CUP OLIVE OIL
1 TEASPOON KOSHER SALT
1/8 TEASPOON GROUND WHITE PEPPER
1/4 CUP WHITE WINE

1. In a bowl large enough to hold the lobster medallions, combine the lemon juice, oil, salt, white pepper and wine. Marinate the lobster tail medallions in this marinade for 30 minutes while refrigerated.
2. Preheat a grill to high heat.
3. Grill the marinated tail medallions over high heat, turning as needed and basting with a small amount of champagne vinaigrette just before the pieces are finished and removed. Keep the tail medallions warm for assembly.

CHAMPAGNE LEMON VINAIGRETTE

1 CLOVE GARLIC, FINELY CHOPPED
2 TABLESPOONS DIJON MUSTARD
1/4 CUP CHAMPAGNE VINEGAR
2 TABLESPOONS LEMON JUICE
1 TEASPOON LEMON ZEST
2 TABLESPOONS GRANULATED SUGAR
1/2 TEASPOON KOSHER SALT
1/2 TEASPOON FRESHLY GROUND BLACK PEPPER
1/4 CUP OLIVE OIL
1/4 CUP CANOLA OIL

1. Whisk together the garlic, mustard, vinegar, lemon juice, lemon zest, sugar, salt and pepper in a large bowl.
2. Slowly whisk in the oils until the dressing is emulsified.** (Alternatively, you can blend all of the ingredients until they form a smooth puree.)

FRISÉE AND RADISH SALAD

2 HEADS BABY FRISÉE, CLEANED AND CRISPED†
OLIVE OIL, TO TASTE
CHAMPAGNE VINAIGRETTE (OPPOSITE PAGE)
KOSHER SALT, TO TASTE
GROUND BLACK PEPPER, TO TASTE
3 RADISHES, SLICED VERY THINLY ON A MANDOLINE,
   TO GARNISH

1. Cut the frisée into small, sprig-like pieces and then dress them lightly with olive oil and champagne vinaigrette and season to taste with salt and pepper.
2. Garnish the presented salad with radish slices.

DILL OIL

¼ CUP DILL (AS MANY FRONDS AS POSSIBLE,
   BUT ALSO STEMS, IF NEEDED)
2 TABLESPOONS CANOLA OIL
SEA SALT, TO TASTE

1. Prepare a bowl of ice water.
2. Blanch the dill in boiling water for 30 seconds and then quickly drain and shock the herbs in the ice water. Strain the water and pat the dill dry with a clean towel.
3. Puree with the canola oil in a blender.
4. Strain the oil and season to taste with salt.

ASSEMBLY: For serving, choose a canvas option that allows for a side-by-side eating experience. A small vessel for the soup will be needed. Garnish the soup with the butter-poached claw as well as a small piece of caramelized fennel. The salad is a small ball of the frisée garnished with the radish slices. Stack or fan out the grilled lobster medallions and finish them with a drizzle of the vinaigrette and dill oil. The fennel flavor in the soup is linked to the salad through the light dill tones that are present from the oil.

*Meaning "white butter," this classic French sauce is composed of wine reduction into which chunks of cold butter are whisked until the sauce is thick and smooth.

**If there is some open champagne — as a pairing, perhaps — add a small amount of champagne to the dressing just before service.

†Place frisée in ice water for 5 minutes

WINE
CHARDONNAY. A California chardonnay is preferred, aged in French oak barrels, with vibrant notes of green apple and melon, and elements of vanilla and toasted oak (imparted from the oak barrels), with a rich, buttery mouthfeel. Cakebread Chardonnay from Napa Valley is a fantastic pairing.

BEER
GERMAN HEFEWEIZEN. A light-bodied wheat beer, hefeweizen has a hazy, bright orange color with a nose of clove and banana that's followed by a dry and restrained bitterness, which lends to a refreshing and clean finish. The hefeweizen from the Schneider Weiss brewery, located north of Munich, is a highly recommended pairing.

pork and apples
WILD BOAR SAUSAGE, CARAMELIZED CORN PANCAKE, FUJI APPLE BUTTER
SLOW-BRAISED PORK SHANK, CIDER REDUCTION, APPLE SLAW
APPLE WOOD BACON-WRAPPED PORK TENDERLOIN, SWEET POTATO HASH, APPLE
    WALNUT CHUTNEY
SERVES 10

WILD BOAR SAUSAGE

3 WILD BOAR SMOKED SAUSAGES*

1. Pan-sear the boar sausage over medium heat or warm the
sausage on a medium-heat grill.
2. Let the meat rest for 5 minutes before slicing and serving.

CORN PANCAKE

3 EARS CORN, HUSKED
1/3 CUP ALL-PURPOSE FLOUR
1 TEASPOON BAKING POWDER
2 TABLESPOONS GRANULATED SUGAR
KOSHER SALT, TO TASTE
1/4 CUP WHOLE MILK
2 MEDIUM-SIZE EGGS
2 TABLESPOONS VEGETABLE OIL, OR AS NEEDED
ACCOMPANIMENT: PURE MAPLE SYRUP

1. Simmer the corn in boiling water until it is tender (about 5 minutes) and then transfer the ears to ice water to set the texture. Remove from water and pat dry with towel.
2. Whisk together the flour, baking powder, and sugar. Season to taste with salt.
3. Cut enough kernels from the cobs to measure 2 cups.
4. In a separate bowl, whisk the milk and eggs and then add the corn kernels, whisking until just combined.
5. Fold in the dry ingredients to the wet ingredients, combining them well.
6. Heat a griddle or heavy skillet over medium heat until it is hot; lightly brush with oil. Working in batches, spoon 1-2 tablespoons of the batter per pancake onto the griddle and cook until bubbles appear on the surface and the undersides are golden brown (about 2 minutes). The pancakes should be about 2 inches in diameter.
7. Flip with a spatula and cook until the undersides are golden brown (about 1 minute more). (Reduce the heat if the pancakes brown too quickly.)
8. Repeat to cook all of the pancakes, using the rest of the batter; lightly oil the griddle between batches, if necessary. Keep warm until time to serve.

FUJI APPLE BUTTER

3 POUNDS FUJI APPLES, CORED AND ROUGHLY CHOPPED
1 1/2 CUPS APPLE CIDER
1 CUP GRANULATED SUGAR
2 TABLESPOONS LEMON JUICE
1 CUP BROWN SUGAR
1 TEASPOON CINNAMON

1. Combine all of the apple butter ingredients in a heavy stainless-steel saucepan.
2. Bring to a boil over medium-high heat, stirring occasionally.
3. Reduce to a simmer.
4. Once the apples are tender, puree the mixture with a stick blender or use a food processor, working in small batches. Continue cooking gently until the mixture is very thick.
5. Chill before serving.

pork and apples

WILD BOAR SAUSAGE, CARAMELIZED CORN PANCAKE, FUJI APPLE BUTTER
SLOW-BRAISED PORK SHANK, CIDER REDUCTION, APPLE SLAW
APPLE WOOD BACON-WRAPPED PORK TENDERLOIN, SWEET POTATO HASH, APPLE WALNUT CHUTNEY

SLOW-BRAISED PORK SHANK

6 PORK SHANK PIECES (2 1/2 INCHES THICK EACH)
KOSHER SALT, TO TASTE
GROUND BLACK PEPPER, TO TASTE
2 TABLESPOONS EXTRA-VIRGIN OLIVE OIL
2 LARGE CARROTS, CHOPPED
1 LARGE ONION, CHOPPED
5 LARGE CLOVES GARLIC, CHOPPED
1 TABLESPOON CHOPPED FRESH THYME
1 CUP CHICKEN BROTH
1 CUP APPLE CIDER
1/2 CUP BOURBON

1. Preheat oven to 350 degrees.
2. Sprinkle the pork shanks with salt and pepper, to taste.
3. Heat the oil in a heavy, wide pot over medium-high heat. Working in batches, sear the shanks until they are brown on both sides (about 12 minutes per batch); transfer the shanks to a baking sheet.
4. Add the carrots, onion, garlic, and thyme to the pot. Saute until the onion softens (about 5 minutes).
5. Add the broth, apple cider, and bourbon.
6. Return the shanks to the pot. Bring to a boil, scraping up browned bits from bottom of the pan.
7. Cover the pot and place it in the oven. Braise until the pork shanks are tender (about 1 hour, 40 minutes).
8. Remove the shanks very carefully and chill them.
9. Strain the braising liquid and chill it in the refrigerator; discard the solids.
10. Once the stock is chilled, remove the solidified fat that has settled on the surface.
11. Return the stock to the pot and reduce it over medium heat by half its volume. Reserve the reduction to use in the apple cider reduction recipe that follows.
12. When you are ready to serve, warm the shanks in a covered pan in a 250-degree oven with a small amount of the reserved stock.

CIDER REDUCTION

4 CUPS APPLE CIDER
2 CUPS BROWN SUGAR
1 CUP PORK BRAISING REDUCTION (FROM ABOVE)
KOSHER SALT, TO TASTE
GROUND BLACK PEPPER, TO TASTE

1. In heavy saucepan, reduce all of the cider reduction ingredients until a glaze forms (about 1 hour).**
2. Season to taste with salt and pepper.

APPLE SLAW

1 TABLESPOON CIDER VINEGAR
1 TABLESPOON OLIVE OIL
1 TABLESPOON LEMON JUICE
1 TABLESPOON PURE MAPLE SYRUP
1 TABLESPOON WHISKY
1 VERY LARGE GRANNY SMITH APPLE, HALVED, CORED, AND CUT INTO MATCHSTICK-SIZE STRIPS (ABOUT 1 1/2 CUPS)
1/4 CUP VERY FINELY SHREDDED RED CABBAGE
1/4 CUP PAPER-THIN SLICES RED ONION
1 GREEN ONION, VERY THINLY SLICED ON THE BIAS†
KOSHER SALT, TO TASTE
GROUND WHITE PEPPER, TO TASTE

1. Whisk together the vinegar, oil, lemon juice, syrup, and whisky in a medium-size bowl to blend.
2. Mix in the apple, cabbage, red onion, and green onion.
3. Season the slaw to taste with salt and pepper.
4. Refrigerate 1 to 4 hours before serving, tossing occasionally.

GRILLED BACON-WRAPPED PORK TENDERLOIN

10 PORK TENDERLOIN MEDALLIONS (CENTER CUT, 3 OUNCES EACH)
KOSHER SALT, TO TASTE
GROUND BLACK PEPPER, TO TASTE
10 SLICES APPLE WOOD-SMOKED BACON

1. Preheat grill to high heat.
2. Lightly season the pork to taste with salt and pepper.
3. Wrap each tenderloin tightly in a slice of bacon, overlapping the bacon to use the whole piece. Use a small skewer, trussing needle, or toothpick to tightly fasten the bacon.
4. On the hot grill, mark the tenderloin on the flesh sides (top and bottom). Allow for some rendering on the bacon but concentrate specifically on grilling accents onto the meat.
5. Keeping the tenderloins on edge, place them into a skillet over medium heat and finish rendering the bacon on all sides.
6. Finish cooking the tenderloins in the skillet to 140 degrees internal temperature. Rest for about 5 minutes before serving.

APPLE WALNUT CHUTNEY

1 POUND TART GREEN APPLES (SUCH AS GRANNY SMITH),
  PEELED, CORED, AND CHOPPED INTO 1/2-INCH DICE
WATER, AS NEEDED
3 TABLESPOONS LEMON JUICE
1 CUP APPLE CIDER VINEGAR
1 CUP GRANULATED SUGAR
2 TABLESPOONS UNSALTED BUTTER
2 LARGE CLOVES GARLIC, MINCED
1 TABLESPOON PEELED, COARSELY CHOPPED FRESH GINGER
1/2 TABLESPOON GROUND BLACK PEPPER
1 CUP SHELLED WALNUTS, ROASTED
1 1/2 TEASPOONS KOSHER SALT

1. After apples are diced, submerge them in water with lemon juice to prevent browning.
2. Bring the vinegar and sugar to a boil in a large, heavy saucepan, stirring until the sugar dissolves. Reduce the heat and simmer for 10 minutes. Remove from heat.
3. In a large nonstick skillet, melt the butter over medium heat.
4. Add the apples and caramelize slightly (about 5 minutes).
5. Add the garlic, ginger, black pepper, and vinegar mixture. Simmer until the apples are just tender.
6. Remove from heat and add the roasted walnuts, then season the chutney with salt.
7. Place in a bowl and allow it to cool. Cover and chill in the refrigerator. (Can be made 1 week ahead. Keep chilled).

SWEET POTATO HASH

1 1/2 POUNDS RED-SKINNED SWEET POTATOES (YAMS),
  PEELED AND CUT INTO 1/2-INCH CUBES (ABOUT 3 CUPS)
KOSHER SALT, TO TASTE
3 TABLESPOONS CANOLA OIL
1/2 CUP RED ONION BRUNOISE ‡
1/4 CUP PACKED LIGHT BROWN SUGAR
1/4 CUP UNSALTED BUTTER, CHOPPED
GROUND BLACK PEPPER, TO TASTE
2 TABLESPOONS FINELY CHOPPED CHIVES

1. Cook the potatoes in a large pot of boiling salted water until they are slightly softened (about 5 minutes).
2. Drain and then rinse under cold water to cool; drain again.
3. Preheat a large, heavy skillet over medium-high heat. Add the canola oil and onions. Saute until they are golden brown (about 5 minutes).
4. Add the potatoes to the skillet, spreading them in an even layer and pressing with the back of a spoon or spatula. Cook until the potatoes are golden brown, turning them occasionally (about 10 minutes).
5. Add the brown sugar and butter. Continue caramelizing the hash for about 5 minutes.
6. Season to taste with salt and pepper.
7. Remove from heat and gently blend in the fresh chives. Keep warm for plating.

ASSEMBLY: For this dish, lay out the items in a way that allows diners to comfortably move into and through the items as they choose. Keep in mind that the portions should be small because of the abundance of items to eat. Correctly plated, all of the parts should present as one portion, even though there are three different concepts. The pork components on this dish are very different in texture and technique. The apple flavors are also all over the spectrum, especially when it comes to texture. This is what makes this dish so spectacular.

Serve the corn pancake warm, topped with apple butter and sliced wild boar sausage, finishing it with a drizzle of maple syrup. Next, place the shank nestled into a small portion of apple slaw, dripping with apple cider reduction. Finally, set the bacon-wrapped tenderloin atop the sweet potato hash; spoon the apple chutney right over the top. The cider reduction ties together the entire dish, slipping from one item to the next. Eaten in its entirety, this dish is near perfection.

*I suggest using Broken Arrow Ranch smoked sausage. Visit brokenarrowranch.com for more information.

**When a sugar reduction is hot, its viscosity is very thin. A good way to test this is to put a small plate into the refrigerator and chill it. Once you think the reduction is close to having the right consistency, remove the plate from the refrigerator and drizzle the syrup onto the plate. It will cool the syrup immediately and you are able to see if it needs to be reduced more or if it is the consistency of syrup.

† "Bias" refers to cutting at an angle.

‡ A "brunoise" cut refers to cutting the ingredient first into 1/8-inch matchsticks and then into 1/8-inch cubes.

WINE
GERMAN RIESLING. The Auslese variety is medium-bodied and semi-sweet, and exudes vibrant notes of honey, apple, peach, and apricot, with a crisp, refreshing mouthfeel and a slight minerality of gravel and loam on the finish.

BEER
WEIZEN DOPPLEBOCK. Schneider & Sohn Aventinus doppelbock, in particular, is a traditional full-bodied, malty German wheat beer, with port-like aromas of raisins, dates, prunes, bananas and cloves, with a slight warming finish.

tuna vs. escolar
SESAME-CRUSTED TUNA, CUCUMBER "KIMCHEE" SALAD, BLACK RICE-CRUSTED ESCOLAR, SEAWEED SALAD, MISO BUTTERSCOTCH, CRISPY MALANGA "NOODLES"

tuna vs. escolar

I CHOSE THESE TWO TYPES OF FISH FOR COMPARISON because escolar is often considered "white tuna," so to me it seemed natural to pair the two. Tuna tends to be bolder, stronger in flavor, with more depth. Escolar, on the other hand, tends to be lighter, with a cleaner flavor, and the texture is a little softer. It is more delicate and subtle. You might expect those differences by looking at the two types of fish, but let your mouth be the judge.

SESAME-CRUSTED TUNA, CUCUMBER "KIMCHEE" SALAD

SESAME-CRUSTED TUNA

1/4 CUP WHITE SESAME SEEDS
1/4 CUP BLACK SESAME SEEDS
10 2-OUNCE PORTIONS SASHIMI-GRADE TUNA
FINE GROUND SEA SALT, TO TASTE
GROUND BLACK PEPPER, TO TASTE
2 TABLESPOONS CANOLA OIL

1. Preheat a medium-size skillet over high heat.
2. Combine the sesame seeds in a shallow bowl.
3. Season the tuna to taste with salt and pepper and then roll it in the sesame seeds, coating it well.
4. Sear the tuna in the canola oil on all sides (approximately 30 seconds per side). Work in batches to avoid overcrowding the tuna in the pan.
5. Remove from heat and allow the fish to rest for 5 minutes before slicing or serving. (You will be serving the tuna rare.)

CUCUMBER "KIMCHEE" SALAD*

1 ENGLISH CUCUMBER
1 SMALL RED ONION, FINELY JULIENNED
1/4 CUP DISTILLED RICE WINE VINEGAR
1/4 CUP SUGAR
1 TABLESPOON SOY SAUCE
1 TEASPOON THAI CHILI SAUCE
1 TABLESPOON MIRIN
3 TABLESPOONS SESAME OIL
1 CUP FINELY SHREDDED RED CABBAGE
1 SMALL THAI RED PEPPER, VERY FINELY JULIENNED
SALT AND PEPPER, TO TASTE

1. Halve the cucumber lengthwise and remove the seeds. Thinly slice it crosswise.
2. Transfer cucumber and onion to a bowl.
3. In a small saucepot, heat the vinegar and sugar until the sugar dissolves; let cool to room temperature.
4. Add the soy sauce, chili sauce, mirin, and sesame oil to the onion and cucumber.
5. In a separate bowl, combine the cabbage and Thai red pepper and then incorporate the soy mixture into the salad.
6. Season to taste with salt and pepper. Cover and let the flavors marry for 2 hours.

BLACK RICE-CRUSTED ESCOLAR, SEAWEED SALAD

BLACK RICE-CRUSTED ESCOLAR

1 CUP FORBIDDEN BLACK RICE**
10 2-OUNCE PORTIONS SASHIMI-GRADE ESCOLAR
KOSHER SALT, TO TASTE
FRESHLY GROUND WHITE PEPPER, TO TASTE
2 TABLESPOONS CANOLA OIL

1. In a coffee grinder, grind the rice into a fine powder.
2. Place the rice powder in a shallow bowl.
3. Preheat a medium skillet over high heat.
4. Season the escolar to taste with salt and pepper and then press the top side of the fish into the rice powder.
5. Sear the escolar in the canola oil on all sides (approximately 30 seconds per side). Work in batches to avoid overcrowding the pan.
6. Remove from heat and allow the fish to rest for 5 minutes before slicing or serving. (You will be serving the escolar rare.)

SESAME SEAWEED SALAD

3/4 OUNCE DRIED WAKAME SEAWEED (WHOLE)
WARM WATER, AS NEEDED
3 TABLESPOONS RICE VINEGAR (NOT SEASONED)
3 TABLESPOONS SOY SAUCE
2 TABLESPOONS ASIAN SESAME OIL
1 TEASPOON GRANULATED SUGAR
1 TEASPOON PEELED, FINELY GRATED FRESH GINGER
1/2 TEASPOON MINCED GARLIC
2 SCALLIONS, THINLY SLICED
1 TEASPOON THAI CHILI SAUCE
BLACK SESAME SEEDS, TO GARNISH
WHITE SESAME SEEDS, TO GARNISH

1. Place the seaweed in a bowl and cover with warm water, letting it soak for 5 minutes. Drain and then squeeze out the excess water.
2. Finely julienne the seaweed as thinly as possible using a knife.
3. In a bowl, stir together the vinegar, soy sauce, sesame oil, sugar, ginger, and garlic until the sugar is dissolved.
4. Blend in the seaweed, scallions, and chili sauce, tossing well to combine.
5. Sprinkle the salad with sesame seeds before serving.

CRISPY MALANGA NOODLES

2 MEDIUM-SIZED MALANGA, WASHED AND PEELED †
CANOLA OIL, FOR FRYING
SEA SALT, TO TASTE

1. In a large saucepan, heat the canola oil to 350 degrees.
2. While the oil is coming to temperature, use a spiral mandoline or a mandoline with the fine julienne blade to slice the malangas into julienne or strings.
3. Rinse under cold water for 5 minutes to remove the starch. The water at first will be cloudy due to the starch being leached out of it, once the water is clear again all the excess starch has been removed. Drain and then place the pieces onto paper towel and pat dry.
4. Fry the malanga in batches until crisp (about 3 minutes).
5. Season liberally with sea salt, to taste.

MISO BUTTERSCOTCH

3/4 CUP BROWN SUGAR
1/2 CUP CORN SYRUP
2 TABLESPOONS UNSALTED BUTTER
1 CUP HEAVY WHIPPING CREAM
6 TABLESPOONS WHITE MISO PASTE

1. In a medium-size saucepan over medium heat, cook the sugar, corn syrup, butter, and heavy cream until the mixture has a thick consistency.
2. Remove from heat and allow it to cool at room temperature; blend in the miso paste.

ASSEMBLY: Choose a canvas-style plate with some length so you can spread this dish apart a bit. Plate the salad components together with the accompanying fish (tuna with Cucumber "Kimchee" Salad and escolar with the seaweed salad) in a tight configuration. Tie the distance on the plate together with drizzles of the miso butterscotch. Keep the crispy malanga in a contained pile, with access to each item. Offering soy sauce on the side may be a nice touch, possibly in an Asian-style spoon.

* The salad can be prepared in 45 minutes or less but it will need to marinate for at least 2 hours so that the flavors have a chance to develop. This can be made several days ahead of service.

**Forbidden black rice is an heirloom short-grained rice high in fiber and iron. Legend has it that it was once eaten exclusively by Chinese emperors, thus the intriguing name.

†Malangas are corms grown primarily in Central and South America. They look like brown sweet potatoes on the outside, but their flesh is white.

bleu cheese

FIG MARMALADE, CANDIED SPICED WALNUTS, ORGANIC BABY GREENS, PORT WINE VINAIGRETTE

SERVES 10

SELECTION OF BLEU CHEESES

1 POUND FRENCH (ROQUEFORT, GABRIEL COULET LA PETITE CAVE)
1 POUND ENGLISH (STILTON, BOUROUGH MARKET)
1 POUND AMERICAN (BLUE, MAYTAG DAIRY FARMS)

FIG MARMALADE

1 POUND FIGS, WASHED AND CHOPPED
2 CUPS MERLOT WINE
2 1/4 CUPS GRANULATED SUGAR
1 TEASPOON LEMON ZEST
1 TEASPOON ORANGE ZEST

1. In a heavy saucepan, bring the figs and wine to a boil.
2. Add the sugar and simmer until the mixture begins to thicken (about 30 minutes).
3. Add the lemon and orange zests and continue simmering until the mixture is thick (about 10 minutes).
4. Puree the fig mixture in a blender if you prefer a smoother consistency, or smash it with the back of a wooden spoon for a more chunky consistency.
5. Put the marmalade in a container and refrigerate; serve chilled.

PORT WINE VINAIGRETTE

1 CUP TAWNY PORT
2 TABLESPOONS BRUNOISE SHALLOTS*
2 TABLESPOONS GRANULATED SUGAR
2 TABLESPOONS DIJON MUSTARD
3 TABLESPOONS RED WINE VINEGAR
1/4 CUP CANOLA OIL
1/4 CUP OLIVE OIL
KOSHER SALT, TO TASTE
GROUND BLACK PEPPER, TO TASTE

1. Combine the port and shallots in a small, heavy saucepan.
2. Boil until the liquid is reduced to 1/4 cup (about 15 minutes).
3. Remove from heat and allow the mixture to cool.
4. In a blender or using a stick blender, combine the cool port reduction, sugar, mustard, and vinegar; blend well.
5. Stream in the oils while continuing to blend.
6. Season to taste with salt and pepper.

CANDIED SPICED WALNUTS

1 CUP SHELLED WALNUTS
2 TABLESPOONS LIGHT CORN SYRUP
1 TABLESPOON GRANULATED SUGAR
1/2 TEASPOON KOSHER SALT
1/4 TEASPOON GROUND BLACK PEPPER
1/4 TEASPOON GROUND CUMIN
1 GENEROUS PINCH CAYENNE

1. Preheat oven to 325 degrees.
2. Combine all of the ingredients in a medium-size bowl; toss to coat.
3. Spread the mixture on a baking sheet lined with a Silpat or other nonstick baking mat.
4. Bake in the oven, stirring occasionally to break up clumps, until the nuts are deep golden and the sugar mixture is bubbling (about 15 minutes).
5. Let the nuts cool completely on the baking sheet. Once cool, store in an airtight container.

ADDITIONAL INGREDIENTS

4 OUNCES ORGANIC BABY ARUGULA
KOSHER SALT, TO TASTE
CRACKED BLACK PEPPER, TO TASTE

ASSEMBLY: Lightly dress the arugula with the port wine vinaigrette and season to taste with salt and pepper. Portion the cheese into 1- to 2-ounce portions or crumbles and keep separate from each another. Portion the dressed greens onto individual flat plates. Garnish with the candied walnuts and fig marmalade and then drizzle with additional vinaigrette. Finally, place the bleu cheeses separately on the plates. This dish is designed for the bleu cheeses to be tasted and compared to one another, and for the diner to relish the differences and similarities — both large and small. Ultimately, you will recognize that each cheese offers something the other ones do not. Which will be your guests' favorites? Feel free to serve this with some crisps to add to the experience—go ahead, get creative.

WINE
SAUTERNES. Affected by the Noble rot, these raisined grapes have a concentrated sugar content that renders sweet dessert wines, with fragrant aromas of orange blossom and honey and sweet notes of peach, apricot and nectarine. A highly acidic finish keeps the palate in balance and is a fantastic counterpoint to the creaminess of the cheese.

BEER
BARLEY WINE. Barley wine is very strong and complex with aromas of dried fruit, orange and lemon rinds and a sweet and spirituous body of maple syrup, pound cake and caramel. An aged or vintage barley wine, such as the English J.W. Lees, would be the ultimate pairing for this course.

*A "brunoise" cut refers to cutting the ingredient first into
1/8-inch matchsticks and then into 1/8-inch cubes.

a taste of pear
CARAMEL PEAR COBBLER, PORT WINE-POACHED PEAR BUTTER,
PEAR AND CALVADOS ICE CREAM, OVEN-DRIED PEAR CHIPS

OFTEN IT IS A SIMPLE SEASONAL INGREDIENT
that inspires an entire arsenal of flavor profiles. Through
texture and temperature, we are able to create a wide
range of examples of how a simple pear can be exploited.
Creativity plays a large part in my style.

a taste of pear
CARAMEL PEAR COBBLER, PORT WINE-POACHED PEAR BUTTER, PEAR AND CALVADOS ICE CREAM, OVEN-DRIED PEAR CHIPS
SERVES 10

PORT WINE PEAR BUTTER

YIELDS 1 QUART

5 FIRM, RIPE BOSC PEARS, PEELED, CORED, AND
  ROUGHLY CHOPPED
4 CUPS RUBY PORT
1 CUP GRANULATED SUGAR
1 CUP BROWN SUGAR
2 CINNAMON STICKS
1 TABLESPOON LEMON JUICE
1 TEASPOON GROUND CLOVES

1. Place the pears in a saucepan and pour the ruby port over them. Bring to a simmer and reduce port by half.
2. Add the sugar, brown sugar, cinnamon sticks, lemon juice, and ground cloves.
3. Simmer the mixture until the pears are very soft.
4. Remove the cinnamon sticks. Using a stick blender, puree the pears until they are smooth. (You may also transfer the pears and liquid to a food processor to puree.)
5. Continue reducing the mixture over low heat until it is thick.
6. Let it cool before serving.

CARAMEL PEAR COBBLER

3 CUPS PEELED, CORED, AND SMALL-DICED BARTLETT PEARS
1/4 CUP UNSALTED BUTTER
1 CUP DARK BROWN SUGAR
1/4 CUP BOURBON
1 TEASPOON LEMON JUICE
STREUSEL TOPPING, AS NEEDED (RECIPE ON OPPOSITE PAGE)

1. Preheat oven to 425 degrees.
2. In a preheated skillet over medium-high heat, caramelize the diced pears in small batches in a total of 2 tablespoons of butter.
3. Place them in individual ramekins or an appropriately sized casserole dish.
4. Melt the remaining 2 tablespoons of butter over medium-low heat and add the brown sugar. Dissolve the brown sugar, stirring constantly, and then flambé with the bourbon. Be very careful creating this open flame.
5. Add the lemon juice and pour the warm caramel evenly over the diced pears. Top generously with streusel topping, about 1/4 inch on each ramekin.
6. Bake until the top is golden and cobbler is bubbling. Serve hot.

WINE
ICE WINE. Left on the vine to freeze, these grapes have highly concentrated sugar contents that provide intense notes of pear, peach, apricot, and orange blossom, with a sweet mouthfeel and long finish.

CIDER
PEAR CIDER. Light and crisp with champagne-like qualities, this fermented cider is very clean, with fresh pear on the palate and a refreshing, dry finish.

STREUSEL TOPPING

1 1/2 CUPS ALL-PURPOSE FLOUR
1/2 CUP BROWN SUGAR
1/2 TEASPOON NUTMEG
1 TEASPOON GROUND CINNAMON
1/2 CUP UNSALTED BUTTER, SOFTENED
1 TEASPOON VANILLA EXTRACT

1. In a medium bowl, sift the flour, brown sugar, nutmeg, and cinnamon together.
2. Add the butter and vanilla and cut these in until the mixture resembles coarse meal.

PEAR AND CALVADOS ICE CREAM

SERVES 10

2 RIPE PEARS, PEELED, CORED, AND ROUGHLY CHOPPED
1 3/4 CUPS MILK
1/2 CUP HEAVY WHIPPING CREAM
3/4 CUP GRANULATED SUGAR
2 EGGS
3 TABLESPOONS CALVADOS

1. In a saucepan, simmer the pears in milk and cream.
2. Add the sugar and continue simmering until it is dissolved. Using a whisk, break up the pears as much as possible.
3. In a separate bowl, beat the eggs until they are smooth.
4. Temper the eggs by straining the pear-infused cream slowly into the eggs while whisking.

5. Return the mixture to low heat and continue whisking until the custard reaches a nappe consistency.*
6. Remove from heat and stir in the calvados.
7. Cool the mixture and then churn in an ice cream machine until frozen. Store in freezer.

OVEN-DRIED PEAR CHIPS

3 PEARS
FRUIT-FRESH (OPTIONAL)**

1. Preheat oven to 180 degrees.
2. Using a mandoline or slicer, thinly slice the pears lengthwise. Remove the seeds as needed.
3. Lay the slices out on baking sheets lined with a Silpat or nonstick baking mat. If you are using Fruit-Fresh, mix it with a little water and brush this on the pears.
4. Dry them in the oven until crisp (about 2 hours).

ASSEMBLY: Serve this dish as a tasting or a combination dish. The ice cream can be used as the cobbler's "à la mode." The pear chips make a terrific texture garnish and accompany the butter beautifully.

*"Nappe" refers to either the ability of a liquid to coat the back of a spoon or the act of coating a food.

**"Fruit-Fresh" is a Ball brand product that prevents browning of freshly cut produce for up to 8 hours. In this case, it will help the pears from browning while they dry.

chocolate
**DARK CHOCOLATE SOUFFLÉ
ORGANIC CHOCOLATE MILKSHAKE
WHITE HOT CHOCOLATE**

IT IS TYPICAL TO SERVE SAUCE WITH A SOUFFLE,
and that's what I've done here, albeit in a nontraditional
way. The idea is that when the warm souffle comes out of
the oven, and you're ready to dig into it, you have the
option of taking a sip from either one of two drinks on the
side. One, the White Hot Chocolate, is sweet, rich, and
warm. In contrast, the Organic Chocolate Milkshake gives
you the experience of cold ice cream. These beverages are
designed to be the sauce component. But I've also included
a more traditional Vanilla Bean Anglaise, which you can
make instead, if you prefer.

DARK CHOCOLATE SOUFFLÉ

10 OUNCES BITTERSWEET OR SEMISWEET CHOCOLATE,
   FINELY CHOPPED
3/4 CUP HEAVY WHIPPING CREAM
5 TABLESPOONS GRANULATED SUGAR,
   PLUS MORE TO PREPARE RAMEKINS
2 TABLESPOONS UNSALTED BUTTER
1 TABLESPOON DARK RUM
2 TABLESPOONS VANILLA EXTRACT
1/4 TEASPOON KOSHER SALT
6 LARGE EGGS, YOLKS SEPARATED FROM WHITES
PINCH OF CREAM OF TARTAR
POWDERED SUGAR, TO GARNISH

1. Combine the first 7 ingredients (chocolate, cream, sugar,
butter, rum, vanilla, and salt) in a heavy medium-size saucepan.
2. Stir over low heat until the chocolate melts and the mixture
is smooth.
3. Remove from heat and allow it to cool to lukewarm.
(This chocolate base can be made 1 day ahead. Cover and chill.
Stir over low heat just until lukewarm before continuing.)
4. Preheat oven to 350 degrees.
5. Butter 8 3/4-cup ramekins or custard cups and coat the
insides with sugar.
6. Whisk the egg yolks into the lukewarm chocolate base.
7. In a large bowl, use an electric mixer to beat the egg whites
and cream of tartar until soft peaks form.
8. Fold the whites into the chocolate base in 3 additions.
9. Divide the soufflé mixture among the prepared ramekins;
place on a baking sheet.
10. Bake the soufflés in the oven until puffed but still moist in
the center (about 15 minutes).
11. Sift the powdered sugar over the soufflés to garnish and
then serve immediately.

VANILLA BEAN ANGLAISE (OPTIONAL)*

1/2 CUP WHOLE MILK
1/2 CUP HEAVY WHIPPING CREAM
2 INCHES VANILLA BEAN, SPLIT
3 LARGE EGG YOLKS
3 TABLESPOONS GRANULATED SUGAR

1. Combine the milk and heavy whipping cream in a heavy
medium-size saucepan.
2. Scrape in the seeds from the vanilla bean and then add the
bean, too.
3. Bring the milk mixture to a simmer. Remove from heat.
4. In a medium-size bowl, whisk the egg yolks and sugar to
blend them together.
5. Gradually whisk the hot milk mixture into the yolk mixture,
stirring constantly to prevent the eggs from curdling. Return
the custard to the saucepan.
6. Stir over low heat — do not boil — until the custard thickens
(about 5 minutes). It has reached the right consistency when
you can coat the back of a spoon with the custard; draw your
finger across it, and it should leave a path.
7. Strain the sauce into a bowl. Cover and chill. (Can be made 1
day ahead.)

chocolate
DARK CHOCOLATE SOUFFLÉ
ORGANIC CHOCOLATE MILKSHAKE
WHITE HOT CHOCOLATE
SERVES 8

ORGANIC CHOCOLATE MILKSHAKE

1 CUP ORGANIC DARK CHOCOLATE CHIPS
1 CUP HEAVY WHIPPING CREAM
2 CUPS ORGANIC CHOCOLATE MILK
4 SCOOPS CHOCOLATE ICE CREAM

1. Melt the chocolate and heavy cream together over low heat until smooth, stirring frequently.
2. Chill at room temperature.
3. In a blender, combine the chocolate mixture, chocolate milk, and ice cream and blend until smooth. Adjust the consistency with additional chocolate milk if needed. Serve in a frozen glass.

WHITE HOT CHOCOLATE

1 CUP WHITE CHOCOLATE CHIPS
1 CUP HEAVY WHIPPING CREAM
4 CUPS HALF-AND-HALF
1 TEASPOON VANILLA EXTRACT
1/2 CUP WHITE CHOCOLATE LIQUEUR (OPTIONAL)**
VANILLA BEAN WHIPPED CREAM, TO GARNISH (RECIPE BELOW)

1. In a medium-size saucepan over medium heat, combine the white chocolate chips and heavy cream.
2. Stir constantly until the white chocolate chips have completely melted.
3. Stir in the half-and-half, vanilla extract, and chocolate liqueur. Stir occasionally until it is heated through.
4. Keep warm until time to serve. Pour into mugs and top with a dollop of vanilla bean whipped cream.

VANILLA BEAN WHIPPED CREAM

1/2 CUP HEAVY WHIPPING CREAM
3 TABLESPOONS GRANULATED SUGAR
1 VANILLA BEAN, SPLIT AND SCRAPED

1. Place all ingredients in a small mixing bowl.
2. Whip vigorously using a whisk until medium soft peaks form. Keep chilled until assembly.

ASSEMBLY: The approach to this chocolate experience is indeed a tasting. We want to lay out these items in a way that compels diners to taste their way along in whatever order they desire. Actually, the soufflé anchors our plate, and the rich, hot cup of cocoa or the cold, creamy milkshake acts as a nontraditional sauce for the soufflé. If you're just making soufflés, serve with the Vanilla Bean Anglaise.

*The crème anglaise is only necessary if you intend to just make soufflés without the accompanying drinks.

**Godiva has a nice white chocolate liqueur.

WINE
SHERRY. Sherries are fortified wines made from white grapes in Spain. The Oloroso variety is the best compliment for this dessert, with its dark color and rich flavor. With notes of nuts on the nose, particularly walnut, it has a caramel-like flavor that will accent and play against the chocolate in the dish.

BEER
LAMBIC (RASPBERRY OR BLACKBERRY). Tart and dry on the finish, lambic ales can display wild notes of raspberry and other red-seeded fruits, and even funky notes of barnyard, wet dog, and horse blanket; yet they are extremely refreshing. This is an excellent contrast to the heavy notes of the chocolate and will help lift the palate.

experience

THE FOLLOWING RECIPES ARE DESIGNED TO HIGHLIGHT AND ACCENTUATE THE ROLE THAT ALL THE SENSES, AND THE PHYSICAL PROCESS OF DINING, CAN PLAY IN THE ENJOYMENT OF EATING.

TASTE IS OBVIOUSLY A VERY IMPORTANT PART OF eating. But often overlooked, and almost as important, are the other senses and the overall experience of the meal. Smell, in particular, has long influenced my approach to cooking and is something I emphasize in the following recipes. As you will see, sometimes an element can greatly enhance a dish only by adding smell, and without being eaten at all. Rosemary can be a powerful herb, so I recommend using it sparingly for flavor in the recipe for Rosemary-Scented Venison. But the aroma of the herb comes to the forefront by using a large sprig of fresh rosemary that you hold to your nose while eating the venison. The approach gives you control as a diner: If you really like rosemary, you can take big whiffs while you eat; if not, you can just take a little hit. In another example, the recipe for Wagyu Beef Nachos emphasizes sound as well as smell: The meat can be served on a hot river rock, which produces a lively sizzle as well as an enticing aroma. In this presentation, the process of dining is also important, because it allows diners to custom-build their nachos on their own plates. All in all, each recipe in this chapter proves there is more to a meal than just eating the food. (Of course, they still taste great, too.)

"there is more to a meal than just eating the food."

shellfish shooters

ORANGE-SEARED SHRIMP, BLOOD ORANGE MANGO NECTAR
GRILLED LOBSTER TAIL, GRAPEFRUIT AND YUZU EMULSION
CORNMEAL-FRIED OYSTERS, WATERMELON BROTH, HABANERO AIOLI
LUMP CRAB, AVOCADO SOUP, LIME VINAIGRETTE, JALAPENO SALT
SERVES 10

HERE'S A RECIPE FOR ALL YOU SHELLFISH LOVERS...
Make anyone of these shooters or all of them. Take just the
shrimp and crab to a party and serve them tapas-style. Or
serve them all as a starter at a multi-course dinner. Line
'em up and knock 'em down!

1.

1

**ORANGE-SEARED SHRIMP,
BLOOD ORANGE MANGO NECTAR**

BLOOD ORANGE MANGO NECTAR

1 MANGO, PEELED AND CHOPPED (PIT RESERVED)
1 CUP ORANGE JUICE
1 TABLESPOON HONEY
1 TABLESPOON LEMON JUICE
1 TEASPOON CHOPPED FRESNO CHILI
20 BLOOD ORANGE SEGMENTS

1. Place all of the ingredients (including the mango pit) except
the blood orange segments in a small saucepan and simmer
for 10 minutes.
2. Remove the mango pit from the liquid and puree in a blender.
3. Strain the nectar through a fine-mesh sieve.
4. Allow the mixture to cool before serving.
5. Reserve the blood orange segments for service.

2.

4.

3.

shellfish shooters

ORANGE-SEARED SHRIMP, BLOOD ORANGE MANGO NECTAR
GRILLED LOBSTER TAIL, GRAPEFRUIT AND YUZU EMULSION
CORNMEAL-FRIED OYSTERS, WATERMELON BROTH, HABANERO AIOLI
LUMP CRAB, AVOCADO SOUP, LIME VINAIGRETTE, JALAPENO SALT

ORANGE DUST

2 ORANGES
1 CUP WATER
1/3 CUP SUGAR

1. Preheat oven to 200 degrees.
2. Using a sharp knife, carefully remove the zest of the orange, keeping the pieces as large and intact as possible and being careful not to include any of the pulp. (There should be no white pulp on the backside of the zest. If there is some, carefully remove it with a sharp knife.)
3. Once all of the zest has been harvested, bring the water and sugar to a boil in a medium-size saucepan.
4. Simmer the orange zest pieces in the simple syrup mixture for 5 minutes.
5. Remove them from the syrup and drain. Reserve the orange-flavored simple syrup for the orange-seared shrimp preparation.
6. Spread the zest onto a baking sheet and dry in the oven until it is crisp.
7. Allow to cool.
8. Grind in a coffee grinder until it forms a fine powder and store in an airtight container.

ORANGE-SEARED SHRIMP

10 31/40-SIZE SHRIMP, PEELED AND DEVEINED, TAIL REMOVED
SEA SALT, TO TASTE
GROUND WHITE PEPPER, TO TASTE
2 TEASPOONS ORANGE DUST (RECIPE FROM ABOVE)
1 TABLESPOON UNSALTED BUTTER
1/2 CUP ORANGE-FLAVORED SYRUP (RESERVED FROM DUST PREPARATION ABOVE)

1. Split the shrimp end to end and season them with sea salt, pepper, and the orange dust.
2. Preheat a skillet over medium heat.
3. Pan-sear the shrimp in butter, turning as necessary. Just before the shrimp are finished, deglaze the pan with the orange syrup.
4. Remove from heat and assemble shooters immediately (assembly below).

2

GRILLED LOBSTER TAIL, GRAPEFRUIT AND YUZU EMULSION

GRILLED LOBSTER TAIL

1 COLDWATER LOBSTER TAIL (14 OUNCES)
1 TEASPOON LEMON JUICE
1/8 CUP OLIVE OIL
1/4 TEASPOON KOSHER SALT
PINCH GROUND WHITE PEPPER
1 TABLESPOON WHITE WINE

1. Bring a large pot of water to a rolling boil.
2. Place the lobster tail into the boiling water and cook them for 1-2 minutes.
3. Remove and place in ice water.
4. Once it is cold, split it lengthwise with a knife and remove the meat and the vein.
5. In a large mixing bowl, combine the remaining ingredients to make a marinade. Marinate the tail for 10 minutes.
6. Preheat grill to medium-high heat.
7. Grill the tail until just done (about 3-4 minutes per side).
8. Rest the tail for 3 minutes and then slice into small medallions.

GRAPEFRUIT AND YUZU EMULSION

1 CUP GRAPEFRUIT JUICE
3 TABLESPOONS YUZU JUICE
1 TEASPOON SUGAR
1 TABLESPOON GRAPESEED OIL

1. Place the juices and sugar in a bowl to dissolve the sugar.
2. Add oil and froth the mixture with a speed frother or blender.
3. Strain through a fine-mesh sieve. Serve immediately.

3

CORNMEAL-FRIED OYSTERS, WATERMELON BROTH, HABANERO AIOLI

CORNMEAL-FRIED OYSTERS

6 CUPS VEGETABLE OIL
1 LARGE EGG
1/4 CUP WHOLE MILK
2 1/2 TEASPOONS SALT
1 1/2 CUPS CORNMEAL
1/4 TEASPOON GROUND BLACK PEPPER
1 CUP STANDARD-SIZE SHUCKED OYSTERS, DRAINED (ABOUT 18)

1. Heat the oil in a deep, heavy pot over high heat until it reaches 375 degrees using a deep-fat thermometer (about 10 minutes).

2. While the oil is heating, whisk together the egg, milk, and 1 teaspoon of the salt in a bowl.

3. Sift the cornmeal, remaining $1^{1}/_{2}$ teaspoons of salt, and pepper into a separate bowl.

4. Working in batches, add the oysters to the egg mixture; lift out the oysters, letting excess liquid drip off, and then transfer them to the seasoned cornmeal. Coat the oyster on all sides.

5. Knock off any excess coating and carefully transfer to the oil to fry, turning occasionally, until golden and just cooked through (1-2 minutes).

6. Transfer with a slotted spoon to paper towels to drain.

7. Coat and fry the remaining oysters in the same manner, returning the oil to 375 degrees for each batch.

shellfish shooters

ORANGE-SEARED SHRIMP, BLOOD ORANGE MANGO NECTAR
GRILLED LOBSTER TAIL, GRAPEFRUIT AND YUZU EMULSION
CORNMEAL-FRIED OYSTERS, WATERMELON BROTH, HABANERO AIOLI
LUMP CRAB, AVOCADO SOUP, LIME VINAIGRETTE, JALAPENO SALT

HABANERO AIOLI

1 HABANERO PEPPER
1 CUP MAYONNAISE
1 TEASPOON LIME JUICE
1 TEASPOON LIME ZEST
SEA SALT, TO TASTE

1. Place habanero onto a preheated grill over medium-high heat or on an open flame from the burner on the stove. Allow the skin to blister and char while rotating it often with tongs. About 2 minutes per side. Allow to cool.
2. Remove seeds and stem from the habanero.
3. Using a stick blender, puree the mayonnaise and habanero until smooth.
4. Stir in the lime juice and zest.
5. Adjust flavor to taste with sea salt.

WATERMELON BROTH

4 CUPS PEELED, CHOPPED WATERMELON (SEEDLESS)
1/4 CUP GRANULATED SUGAR
1 TEASPOON CHIPOTLE POWDER
SEA SALT, TO TASTE

1. Puree the watermelon in a blender until it is smooth.
2. Strain through a chinois (very fine china cap), collecting the juice in a saucepan.
3. Once strained, add the sugar and chipotle powder and then bring the liquid to a simmer and cook for 5 minutes.
4. Remove from heat and season to taste with sea salt. Chill before serving.

4
LUMP CRAB, AVOCADO SOUP, LIME VINAIGRETTE, JALAPENO SALT

AVOCADO SOUP

YIELDS 2 CUPS

2 MEDIUM-SIZE AVOCADOES, PITTED, QUARTERED, AND PEELED
1/2 CUP VEGETABLE STOCK OR CHICKEN STOCK
1/4 CUP WHOLE MILK
1 CHOPPED SHALLOT
1 TEASPOON FINELY CHOPPED CILANTRO
2 TABLESPOONS SOUR CREAM
KOSHER SALT, TO TASTE
FINELY GROUND BLACK PEPPER, TO TASTE

1. Blend the avocadoes, stock, milk, shallot, cilantro, and sour cream in a blender until the mixture is smooth.
2. Season the soup to taste with salt and pepper.
3. Adjust consistency with additional stock if needed.

LIME VINAIGRETTE

1 EGG YOLK
1 TEASPOON DIJON MUSTARD
1/4 CUP CHAMPAGNE VINEGAR
1/4 CUP LIME JUICE
1/8 CUP GRANULATED SUGAR
1 TEASPOON LIME ZEST
1 CUP CANOLA OIL
KOSHER SALT, TO TASTE
FINELY GROUND WHITE PEPPER, TO TASTE

1. Using a stick blender, puree the first 6 ingredients until smooth.
2. Stream in the oil while continuing to blend.
3. Season to taste with salt and pepper.

LUMP CRAB

1 8-OUNCE CAN LUMP CRABMEAT (PASTEURIZED)
LIME VINAIGRETTE, AS NEEDED (RECIPE ABOVE)

1. Lightly season the crab in a bowl with the Lime Vinaigrette.
2. Cover and refrigerate for 10 minutes.

JALAPENO SALT*

1 3/4 TEASPOONS KOSHER SALT
1/4 TEASPOON ONION POWDER
1/4 TEASPOON GARLIC POWDER
1 TABLESPOON AND 2 TEASPOONS JALAPENO POWDER**

1. Combine all of the ingredients and store in an airtight container.

ASSEMBLY: First and foremost, the approach to this experience is that there are four distinct options. For each option, there can be some variance in how the shot is rimmed. Using wedges of lemons, limes, oranges, or grapefruits, wet the rim of the shot glass for the coordinating item and dip the rim into salt, dust, or powder. Be creative: Jalapeno salt, sea salt, chipotle powder, and orange dust are some options for rimming the glasses. Fill the shots halfway with the various broths, soups, nectars, and emulsifications. Finish each with its corresponding shellfish component. These shellfish shooters are terrific for tapas-style events. They are also a fun, different way to compare the nuances of seafood and fruit. Line 'em up and knock 'em down.

*You are able to use this spicy salt on just about anything you like to give it just a little different taste.

**Look for jalapeno powder at specialty markets or with online retailers.

WINE
SAUVIGNON BLANC. Crisp and refreshing New Zealand wines with racy acidity and a clean, dry finish, these varietals display notes of floral and herbal grasses on the nose with ripe melon and tropical fruits on the palate. High levels of acidity and a short finish make it a perfect combination for shellfish and seafood, and will compliment the citrus notes of the dish. Marlborough Valley's Cloudy Bay is excellent.

BEER
INDIA PALE ALE. Highly hop-forward; intense, full-flavored mouth feel of orange and grapefruit citrus; fragrant, floral notes on the nose—IPA's are a great contrast to spicy notes in any dish and help to refresh and reset the palate between bites.

tartare
TUNA VS. BEEF
SPICY VS. SWEET
SERVES 8 TASTING SPOONS OF EACH

DON'T LET THE FACT THAT TARTARE IS RAW SCARE YOU off. Even if the thought is unpleasant at first, I urge you with every ounce of my being to try this. Compared to cooked tuna, tartare has a really light texture. And the color alone makes me hungry.

1
BLUEFIN TUNA TARTARE

SPICY

    6 OUNCES BLUEFIN TUNA, BRUNOISE*
    2 TEASPOONS SOY SAUCE
    1 TEASPOON THAI CHILI SAUCE
    1 TEASPOON MINCED CHIVES
    1 TEASPOON SESAME OIL
    SEA SALT, TO TASTE

SWEET

    6 OUNCES BLUEFIN TUNA, BRUNOISE*
    1 1/2 TEASPOONS SOY SAUCE
    1 TEASPOON SWEET PLUM WINE
    1 TEASPOON MIRIN
    1 TEASPOON MINCED CHIVES
    1 TEASPOON SESAME OIL
    SEA SALT, TO TASTE

1.

2
KOBE TARTARE

SPICY

6 OUNCES KOBE BEEF, BRUNOISE*
2 TEASPOONS SOY SAUCE
1 TEASPOON MINCED GINGER
1 TEASPOON MINCED CHIVES
1 TEASPOON SESAME OIL
1 TEASPOON THAI CHILI SAUCE
SEA SALT, TO TASTE

SWEET

6 OUNCES KOBE BEEF, BRUNOISE*
1½ TEASPOONS SOY SAUCE
1 TEASPOON MIRIN
1 TEASPOON PLUM WINE
1 TEASPOON MINCED CHIVES
1 TEASPOON MINCED GINGER
1 TEASPOON SESAME OIL
SEA SALT, TO TASTE

1. For each of the 4 tartare preparations combine all of the ingredients in 4 separate bowls and adjust flavor with sea salt.
2. Let stand to marry flavors for a minimum of 30 minutes, but they taste amazing after 4 hours.

2.

tartare
TUNA VS. BEEF
SPICY VS. SWEET

RED ONION MARMALADE

    3 TABLESPOONS UNSALTED BUTTER
    6 CUPS THINLY JULIENNED RED ONIONS
      (ABOUT 3 1/4 POUNDS)
    1 CUP PACKED DARK BROWN SUGAR
    1/4 CUP RED WINE VINEGAR
    1 CUP RED WINE
    1/2 CUP DRY SHERRY
    KOSHER SALT, TO TASTE
    FINELY GROUND BLACK PEPPER, TO TASTE

1. Melt the butter in a large, heavy pot over medium heat.
2. Add the onions and cook until they are tender, stirring
occasionally (about 30 minutes).
3. Add the brown sugar, vinegar, and red wine.
4. Cook uncovered until the onions are very tender and the
mixture is thick, stirring frequently (about 20 minutes).
5. Add the sherry and continue cooking until mixture is very
thick and dark, stirring frequently.
6. Season to taste with salt and pepper and cool completely.
Cover and refrigerate. (Can be prepared 4 days ahead.)

ADDITIONAL INGREDIENTS

    WASABI, TO GARNISH
    PICKLED GINGER OR BABY PEA SHOOTS, TO GARNISH

ASSEMBLY: When I prepare and serve this dish, I like to use a
vessel that has four different sections or compartments, or to
serve each tartare in an Asian spoon or pedestal sectional for
portability. For the plate, use a small cylindrical mold to form
bite-sized portions.

Place some wasabi alongside the spicy tuna and beef versions.
Pickled ginger or baby pea shoots work beautifully with the
sweet tuna. Finish off the sweet beef version with a small
amount of onion marmalade.

*A "brunoise" cut refers to cutting the ingredient first into
1/8-inch matchsticks and then into 1/8-inch cubes.

WINE
MOURVEDRE. More robust than a pinot noir and lighter than most cabernets or Shirazes, this blend exudes a spicy and gamey nose of barnyard and leather, with a nice tannic structure and flavors of plum and cherry.

BEER
BELGIAN-STYLE WITBIER. Known as "white" beer, these wheat beers are typically spiced with orange peel and coriander and carry a spritzy, light-bodied mouthfeel with a slightly tangy finish. American witbiers would work great here as well, such as the Michigan Brewery Celis White.

smoke & seafood
BOURBON-SCENTED SHRIMP, SMOKY CHIPOTLE REMOULADE
ALDER WOOD SMOKING SCALLOP, CUCUMBER DILL RELISH
SMOKED SALMON BLT, PUMPERNICKEL TOAST, LEMON THYME SMEAR

SERVES 10

THIS DISH MIGHT BE THE "SMOKING GUN" OF YOUR MEAL, so to speak. The experiential element of the dish comes in the form of real, fresh smoke that's trapped in a glass cylinder at each guest's place at the table. (If it sounds cool, that's because it is.) It offers the same effect as if you were dining on a patio with a hardwood smoker going in the background, but it is achieved using a specialty handheld smoker, which isn't common to most household kitchens. There are other smoky elements in the dish as well, such as the Smoked Salmon, the Smoky Chipotle Remoulade, and the Bourbon-Scented Shrimp. (Bourbon is aged in charred barrels.) All together, this dish lets you explore the use of smoke in several different forms.

BOURBON-SCENTED SHRIMP, SMOKY CHIPOTLE REMOULADE

BOURBON-SCENTED SHRIMP

1 TABLESPOON LEMON ZEST
2 TABLESPOONS CANOLA OIL
3 TABLESPOONS BOURBON
GROUND BLACK PEPPER, TO TASTE
10 U16/20 SHRIMP, TAIL ON, PEELED, AND DEVEINED*
SEA SALT, TO TASTE
1 GREEN ONION, CHOPPED, FOR GARNISH

1. In a bowl, mix together the lemon zest, canola oil, and bourbon together and then season to taste with pepper.
2. Marinate the shrimp in this mixture for a minimum of 30 minutes and no longer than 2 hours.
3. Preheat a grill to medium-high heat.
4. Grill the shrimp for two minutes on each side, basting them with the marinade as they cook.
5. To serve, garnish with chopped green onions and then season to taste with sea salt.

WINE
GEWURTZTRAMINER. Medium-bodied with light floral notes on the nose and a sweet and slightly mineral mouthfeel, this wine is big enough to withstand heavier sauces and smoke notes, yet subtle enough not to overpower the seafood.

BEER
SMOKED PORTER. Made with malted barley that has been lightly smoked on wood, these porters have a great roasted and toasty malt backbone with notes of coffee, chocolate, and campfire smoke.

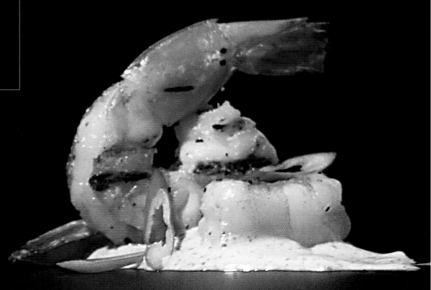

smoke & seafood

BOURBON-SCENTED SHRIMP, SMOKY CHIPOTLE REMOULADE
ALDER WOOD SMOKING SCALLOP, CUCUMBER DILL RELISH
SMOKED SALMON BLT, PUMPERNICKEL TOAST, LEMON THYME SMEAR

SMOKY CHIPOTLE REMOULADE

YIELDS 2 CUPS

3 EGG YOLKS
1/3 CUP VEGETABLE OIL
1/4 CUP CHOPPED GREEN ONIONS
1/8 CUP FRESH PARSLEY LEAVES
2 TABLESPOONS DIJON MUSTARD
1 TABLESPOON WORCESTERSHIRE SAUCE
1 TABLESPOON CHAMPAGNE VINEGAR
1 TABLESPOON TABASCO SAUCE
1 TABLESPOON MINCED GARLIC
2 TABLESPOONS LEMON JUICE
1 TABLESPOON KETCHUP
1 TEASPOON CHIPOTLE POWDER
KOSHER SALT, TO TASTE

1. In a food processor, beat the egg yolks and then stream in the oil while the machine is running.
2. Blend in all of the remaining ingredients until well blended.
3. Adjust the seasoning with salt, as needed.

SMOKING SCALLOP, CUCUMBER DILL RELISH

SMOKING SCALLOP

10 SEA SCALLOPS (10-COUNT SIZE)*
2 TABLESPOONS DRY WHITE WINE
2 TABLESPOONS OLIVE OIL
2 TABLESPOONS UNSALTED BUTTER
HANDHELD SMOKING DEVICE (OPTIONAL)**
ALDER WOOD CHIPS (OPTIONAL)
SEA SALT, TO TASTE

1. Heat a skillet over medium-high heat.
2. Drizzle the scallops with wine and olive oil.
3. Add the butter to the hot skillet and saute the scallops for 3 minutes per side until just cooked, basting them with hot butter from the pan during the final minute of cooking.
4. Remove the scallops from the hot pan and allow them to rest in a container with a tight-fitting lid.†
5. Using a handheld smoking device, blow smoke into the container using alder wood chips and seal container with the lid.
6. Allow the scallops to sit in the trapped smoke for a minimum of 3 minutes and up to 5 minutes.
7. Season to taste with salt just before serving.

CUCUMBER DILL RELISH

1 CUP PEELED AND BRUNOISE ENGLISH CUCUMBER‡
1 TABLESPOON FRESH LEMON JUICE
2 TEASPOONS MINCED DILL
1 TEASPOON CHAMPAGNE VINEGAR
2 TABLESPOONS MINCED RED ONION
1 TEASPOON BRUNOISE ROASTED RED PEPPER‡
1 TEASPOON CAPERS
SEA SALT, TO TASTE
FRESHLY GROUND PEPPER, TO TASTE

1. Mix together all of the relish ingredients and season to taste with salt and pepper.

SMOKED SALMON BLT, PUMPERNICKEL TOAST, LEMON THYME SMEAR

LEMON THYME SMEAR

1 TABLESPOON LEMON ZEST
2 TEASPOONS LEMON JUICE
1 CUP CREAM CHEESE, SOFTENED
1 TEASPOON MINCED FRESH THYME
SEA SALT, TO TASTE

1. Beat together the ingredients until the smear is smooth.

SMOKED SALMON BLT

6 SLICES THICK-CUT APPLE WOOD-SMOKED BACON, CUT LENGTHWISE AND THEN IN HALF
1/2 CUP LEMON THYME SMEAR (RECIPE ABOVE)
10 SLICES PUMPERNICKEL COCKTAIL BREAD, TOASTED
10 SLICES SMOKED SALMON, GENERALLY 1 OUNCE PER SLICE
2 OUNCES BABY ARUGULA
2 ROMA TOMATOES, BRUNOISE‡

1. In a skillet over medium heat, render the bacon until it is crispy.
2. Transfer to a paper towel-lined plate to drain.
3. Build the sandwich by spreading the lemon thyme smear onto freshly toasted pumpernickel bread.
4. Lay down the salmon and then top with arugula, tomato, and crispy bacon.

ASSEMBLY: Use a flat, canvas-style plate with plenty of space for a 3-item dish. Working quickly, choose spaces on the plate for each item and begin putting down the cold components. For example, the smoked salmon blt can be assembled and plated first, because it does not have any components which require last-second heat. Spoon on remoulade sauce for the shrimp and plate a small amount of cucumber relish. Next, place a smoked scallop on the cucumber relish and then, finally, position the freshly grilled bourbon shrimp on the remoulade sauce.

*Shrimp and scallops are sized by the number of them per pound. In this case, it takes 16-20 shrimp and only about 10 scallops to make up 1 pound.

**The handheld smoking device by Poly Science is available through JB Prince Company, New York. It is battery powered and works through a vacuum system.

†I use a cylindrical glass tasting vessel to trap smoke with the scallop when I present this dish. It is appealing to the eyes and the nose when the trapped smoke is released in front of the diner. But the scallops can be served successfully without the use of this technique.

‡A "brunoise" cut refers to cutting an ingredient first into ¹/₈-inch matchsticks and then into ¹/₈-inch cubes.

wild mushroom risotto

PERFECT RISOTTO, MANY GARNISHES OF MUSHROOMS

SERVES 10

PERFECT RISOTTO

6 CUPS VEGETABLE OR CHICKEN STOCK
1 TABLESPOON OLIVE OIL
6 TABLESPOONS UNSALTED BUTTER
1/3 CUP FINELY DICED SHALLOTS
2 CUPS ARBORIO RICE
1/2 CUP DRY WHITE WINE
1 OUNCE DRIED MUSHROOM POWDER
1/2 CUP FRESHLY GRATED PARMIGIANO-REGGIANO CHEESE
KOSHER SALT, TO TASTE
FRESHLY GROUND PEPPER, TO TASTE

1. In a saucepan over medium heat, bring the stock to a simmer.
2. While the stock is coming to a simmer, combine the olive oil and 1 tablespoon of the butter in a heavy 4-quart pot over medium-high heat.
3. Add the shallots and cook until they begin to soften (2-3 minutes; don't allow them to brown).
4. Stir in the rice and cook for 1 minute, stirring to coat well.
5. Add the wine and cook, stirring until the rice mostly absorbs it.
6. Add the mushroom powder and stir to incorporate.
7. Add the simmering broth, 1/2 cup at a time, stirring well after each addition. Wait until each addition is nearly absorbed before proceeding with the next 1/2 cup.
8. When the rice is tender yet firm (about 20 minutes), remove it from heat.
9. Finish the risotto with the remaining 5 tablespoons of the butter and the Parmigiano-Reggiano cheese.
10. Season to taste with salt and pepper.

PAN FRIED MORELS

1/2 CUP ALL-PURPOSE FLOUR
KOSHER SALT, TO TASTE
GROUND BLACK PEPPER, TO TASTE
3 TABLESPOONS UNSALTED BUTTER
10 LARGE MORELS

1. In a medium-size mixing bowl, season the flour generously with salt and pepper.
2. Heat the butter in a large skillet to medium-high heat.
3. Dredge the mushrooms 1 at a time in the flour mixture and knock off any excess flour.
4. Saute them in the butter, rotating as necessary to brown them well and get a crispy texture (about 1 minute per side).

CRISPY ENOKI MUSHROOMS

4 CUPS CANOLA OIL, FOR FRYING
24 OUNCES ENOKI MUSHROOMS, SEPARATED*
1 CUP ALL-PURPOSE FLOUR
KOSHER SALT, TO TASTE

1. Heat the oil in a 2-quart saucepan to 325 degrees.
2. While the oil is coming to temperature, combine the enoki mushrooms and flour in a mixing bowl and coat them well.
3. Working quickly remove excess flour and fry mushrooms in small batches until crispy and golden.
4. Move mushrooms to a paper towel-lined bowl and season to taste with salt.

PORTOBELLO MUSHROOM DUXELLE

2 TABLESPOONS UNSALTED BUTTER
1 TABLESPOON MINCED SHALLOT
16 OUNCES BABY PORTOBELLO MUSHROOMS, STEMMED AND BRUNOISE**
1/2 CUP RED WINE
KOSHER SALT, TO TASTE
FRESH GROUND PEPPER, TO TASTE
1 TABLESPOON MINCED CHIVES

1. In a stainless-steel sauteuse, melt the butter over medium-high heat and sweat the shallot for 2-3 minutes.†
2. Add the portobello mushrooms and cook them for 5 minutes, stirring occasionally.
3. Turn heat to low and add the red wine, letting the liquid reduce completely.
4. Remove from heat, season to taste with salt and pepper, and then garnish the mixture with chives.

ADDITIONAL GARNISHES OF MUSHROOMS

SLICED BLACK TRUFFLE, TO GARNISH
TRUFFLE OIL, TO GARNISH

ASSEMBLY: Choose a vessel that allows diners to experience enjoying the various textures and flavors of the mushrooms components as they choose. As you plate this dish keep the risotto in the center with all the garnishes separated and surrounding the risotto. Drizzle the entire plate with a small bit of truffle oil and sliced truffle to finish.

*Enoki mushrooms are often sold with their root systems still intact. Slice off the root ends and separate the individual mushrooms for this recipe.

**A "brunoise" cut refers to cutting the ingredient first into 1/8-inch matchsticks and then into 1/8-inch cubes.

†A "sauteuse" pan is a straight-sided saute pan.

WINE
BAROLO. Rich and robust Italian reds made in the Piedmont region, these wines exude intense notes of truffles, roses, and ripe strawberries, making them an excellent match for the creamy risotto and earthy mushrooms.

BEER
SCOTCH ALE. Scotch ales are rich and full-bodied with notes of butterscotch, chocolate, smoked peat, caramel, and dark red fruit, and have a slightly bitter finish.

american wagyu beef nachos

SIZZLING BEEF, FRESH FRIED CORN TORTILLA, MICRO CILANTRO SALAD, PICO DE GALLO, JALAPENO QUESO SAUCE

SERVES 8

PICO DE GALLO

1 CUP BRUNOISE TOMATO*
1 TABLESPOON SEEDED AND BRUNOISE JALAPENO*
2 TABLESPOONS BRUNOISE RED ONION*
1 TEASPOON LIME JUICE
1/2 TEASPOON LIME ZEST
KOSHER SALT, TO TASTE
GROUND BLACK PEPPER, TO TASTE

1. Combine all of the ingredients and adjust flavor to taste with salt and pepper.
2. Allow the flavors to marry for at least 1 hour before serving.

JALAPENO QUESO SAUCE

1/4 CUP UNSALTED BUTTER
1/2 CUP ALL-PURPOSE FLOUR
3 CUPS CHICKEN STOCK
3/4 CUP SHREDDED WHITE CHEDDAR CHEESE
3/4 CUP SHREDDED SHARP CHEDDAR CHEESE
3 TABLESPOONS SEEDED AND BRUNOISE JALAPENO*
KOSHER SALT, TO TASTE
GROUND WHITE PEPPER, TO TASTE

1. In a medium saucepot melt the butter over medium heat.
2. Add the flour and stir to form a roux. Reduce heat and cook the roux, keeping it as light as possible.
3. Add the chicken stock and simmer very slowly for 45 minutes.
4. Stir in the shredded cheese and jalapenos. Simmer for 15 more minutes, whisking frequently. Adjust the flavors to taste with salt and pepper.

FRESH FRIED CORN TORTILLA

CANOLA OIL, FOR DEEP-FRYING
20 6-INCH CORN TORTILLAS
KOSHER SALT, TO TASTE
FRESHLY GROUND BLACK PEPPER, TO TASTE

1. Preheat the canola oil to 350 degrees in a deep fryer or large stockpot. (If you are using a pot, keep the oil to no more than half the volume of the pot.)
2. Cut the tortillas into desired size chips (such as triangles) and fry them in the oil in small batches for 2 minutes, until golden brown.
3. Once the chips are crisp, remove them from the pot with a slotted spoon or strainer and place them on a paper towel-lined tray or bowl. Season to taste with salt and pepper while hot. Serve warm.

MICRO CILANTRO GARNISH

1 OUNCE MICRO CILANTRO
LIME VINAIGRETTE, AS NEEDED (RECIPE ON PAGE 80)

1. Dress the cilantro very lightly with lime vinaigrette. (Use this as a garnish element, as it can be very potent.)

WINE	BEER
MALBEC. This varietal, most popular in Argentina, has bold notes of dark berries and spices on the nose, followed by vanilla, blackberry, and more spice on the palate. Big tannins and a medium acidity make wines made from this grape a great match for red meats and spicy foods.	**MÄRZEN.** Amber in color, with bread notes and a caramelized-malt presence, these lagers are juicy and medium-bodied, well-rounded, and very approachable for the domestic-beer drinker.

SIZZLING WAGYU BEEF

1 TEASPOON CHILI POWDER
1 TEASPOON GROUND CUMIN
1 TEASPOON GROUND BLACK PEPPER
½ TEASPOON CHIPOTLE POWDER
½ TEASPOON GARLIC POWDER
½ TEASPOON ONION POWDER
2 POUNDS BONELESS AMERICAN WAGYU BEEF SHORT RIBS
1 TABLESPOON KOSHER SALT
1 TABLESPOON CANOLA OIL

1. Blend all of the dry seasonings together except for the salt.
2. Preheat a skillet over high heat.
3. Season the ribs generously with salt and rub the seasoning blend into the meat.
4. Sear the beef in the canola oil in the hot skillet, creating a nice crust on all sides, turning the meat as needed.
5. Rest the meat to a perfect medium-rare before slicing it thinly for the presentation of the dish.

ASSEMBLY: This experience is not only about flavor, but also sound and smell. I serve the tataki-style Wagyu beef on a hot river rock. It is sizzling when presented — think fajitas. This sizzle produces a fair amount of smell. You also have the experience of building your own nachos, one customized chip at a time. Present this dish in the manner of an assembly line for the diner to enjoy the process. (There are no guarantees that rocks are safe to put into ovens and bring to high temperatures. They can be difficult to work with under these circumstances. Execute with caution. Another option is to bypass this step of the presentation and just serve the seared beef straight away on the plate.)

*A "brunoise" cut refers to cutting the ingredient first into ⅛-inch matchsticks and then into ⅛-inch cubes.

rosemary-scented venison

SLOW-ROASTED VENISON TENDERLOIN, DAUPHINOISE POTATO, CRISPY TOBACCO ONIONS, ROSEMARY AU JUS

SERVES 10

VENISON TENDERLOIN AND ROSEMARY AU JUS

3 POUNDS VENISON TENDERLOINS,
    TRIMMED AND SILVER SKIN REMOVED
KOSHER SALT, TO TASTE
FRESHLY GROUND BLACK PEPPER, TO TASTE
CANOLA OIL, AS NEEDED
1 CUP ROUGHLY CHOPPED ONION
1/2 CUP ROUGHLY CHOPPED CARROT
1/2 CUP ROUGHLY CHOPPED CELERY
4 SPRIGS ROSEMARY
4 CUPS RED WINE
3 CUPS BEEF STOCK

1. Preheat oven to 250 degrees.
2. Heat a heavy-gauge roasting pan over medium-high heat, using 2 burners if necessary.
3. Season the venison to taste with salt and pepper on all sides.
4. Drizzle the heated pan with canola oil and then immediately place the tenderloins in the pan. Sear all sides well (about 2 minutes on each side).
5. Remove the meat and then put the mirepoix vegetables in the roasting pan; allow them to caramelize, stirring as needed.*
6. Remove the pan from heat and create a bed with the mirepoix and rosemary sprigs in the roasting pan, and then place the tenderloins on top.
7. Slow-roast the meat in the oven until the internal temperature reaches 125 degrees.
8. Remove from the oven and allow the tenderloins to rest for a minimum of 5 minutes before slicing.
9. For the jus, strain any fat from the roasting pan and return the pan to medium-high heat with the mirepoix and rosemary.
10. Deglaze the pan with red wine and reduce to 1/2 cup.
11. Remove the rosemary and add the beef stock; reduce by half.
12. Strain through a fine-mesh sieve; keep warm for service.

DAUPHINOISE POTATO

1 TABLESPOON UNSALTED BUTTER, PLUS MORE AS NEEDED
1 CUP FINELY JULIENNED ONION
3 POUNDS IDAHO POTATOES, PEELED AND SLICED
   INTO 1/8-INCH-THICK PIECES
SALT, TO TASTE
PEPPER, TO TASTE
3 CUPS BÉCHAMEL SAUCE, COLD (RECIPE ON PAGE 132)
1/2 CUP GRATED PARMESAN CHEESE
1 CUP GRATED GRUYÈRE CHEESE

1. In a saute pan over medium heat, melt 1 tablespoon of butter and then add the onion. Stir often and allow to cook for 15 minutes or until onions are tender and golden in color.
2. Remove from pan and allow to cool to room temperature.
3. Preheat oven to 350 degrees.
4. Generously butter a 9-inch baking pan.
5. Layer the bottom of the pan with the sliced potatoes and then season to taste with salt and pepper.
6. Coat the potatoes with a thin layer of béchamel sauce and sprinkle with one fourth of each cheese and one fourth of the caramelized onion. Repeat this step until all of the potatoes, béchamel sauce, cheeses, and onion are used, ending with cheese on top.
7. Loosely cover the potatoes with foil and bake in the oven until they are tender (about 45 minutes).
8. Remove the foil and continue baking until the top is browned.
9. Allow the casserole to rest at least 5 minutes before serving.

CRISPY TOBACCO ONIONS†

6 CUPS CANOLA OIL
2 CUPS ALL-PURPOSE FLOUR
2 TABLESPOONS CHIPOTLE POWDER
4 PEELED VIDALIA ONIONS (SMALL ENOUGH IN DIAMETER TO
   FIT ON A MANDOLINE)
SALT, TO TASTE

1. In a 4-quart (or larger) stockpot over medium heat, bring the canola oil to 350 degrees.
2. In a large mixing bowl, blend the flour and chipotle powder.
3. On a mandoline, slice the onions very thinly into rings.
4. Flour the onions as you go in small batches to ensure your flour does not become clumpy due to moisture content. Place the onion slices in the flour mixture and gently coat them, working the rings apart with your fingers.

5. Place the floured onions in a sieve and back over the mixing bowl containing the flour mixture; shake well to remove the excess flour stuck to the onions. Immediately place the onions in the hot oil.
6. Using a long pair of tongs, gently fry the onions until they are crispy and golden.
7. Remove the onions from the oil and transfer to a paper towel-lined pan; season to taste with salt.

ADDITIONAL INGREDIENTS

FRESHLY GRATED HORSERADISH, TO GARNISH
10 LONG, FULL SPRIGS ROSEMARY, FOR AROMATICS

ASSEMBLY: Choose a vessel that will comfortably hold the jus and still have plenty of room to accommodate the other elements of the dish. Place a small portion of potato in the center. Top with thinly sliced venison tenderloin and warm jus. Pile up a generous, airy stack of crispy tobacco onions. Garnish with freshly grated horseradish. Place a large sprig of rosemary on the edge of the vessel or at each person's place setting. Instruct diners to smell the fresh rosemary periodically as they eat through the dish.

*"Mirepoix" refers to a combination of chopped aromatic vegetables, usually two parts onion, one part carrot, and one part celery.

† "Tobacco" gets the name from the smokiness of the chipotle powder detected when eating these deliciously crispy onions.

smoldering s'mores trio

S'MORES TRUFFLE
S'MORES CARAMEL BARK
S'MORES MARTINI

SERVES 12

THE FULL EXPERIENCE OF GRILLING MARSHMALLOWS over an open campfire is difficult to duplicate without the fire. There's something about smelling smoke while eating s'mores that makes them special. This recipe calls for placing leaves in the center of the table and letting them smolder while the dessert is served to invoke that campfire experience. But even without the smoldering leaves, there is plenty about this recipe that makes it an upgrade over the campfire version. The S'mores Truffles, for example, have graham cracker on the outside, with melted chocolate and roasted marshmallow on the inside. Then they're served chilled.

S'MORES TRUFFLES

2 TABLESPOONS UNSALTED BUTTER
½ CUP HEAVY WHIPPING CREAM
2 CUPS MILK CHOCOLATE CHIPS (12 OUNCES)
24 LARGE MARSHMALLOWS (RECIPE ON PAGE 98)
1 CUP FINELY CRUSHED GRAHAM CRACKERS

1. Melt the butter in a medium-size saucepan over medium heat; whisk in the cream and bring it to a boil.
2. Remove the pan from heat and then stir in the chocolate chips until they are melted and smooth. Set aside.
3. Toast the marshmallows over a gas burner or fire, or use a kitchen torch; allow them to cool.
4. Using a toothpick, dip each marshmallow into the chocolate mixture and then dredge in graham cracker crumbs.
5. Chill the truffles before serving.

S'MORES CARAMEL BARK

1 CUP MINI MARSHMALLOWS
24 OUNCES DARK CHOCOLATE, CHOPPED
1 CUP CHOPPED DUTCH CARAMEL WAFER (STROOPWAFEL)*

1. Using a kitchen torch, toast the mini marshmallows.
2. In the top of a double boiler, melt half of the chocolate over low heat until it is just melted.
3. Stir in the second half of the chocolate. (This is known as a vaccination method for tempering chocolate.)**
4. Continue melting the chocolate, stirring frequently as it comes to 88 degrees Fahrenheit on a candy thermometer.
5. Blend in half of the marshmallows and wafers.
6. Spread the mixture as thinly as possible onto a Silpat-lined baking sheet and immediately sprinkle with the remaining marshmallows and wafers.
7. Allow the bark to set and then break it into desired-size pieces. Store in a cool, dry place in an airtight container for up to 2 weeks.

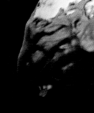

smoldering s'mores trio
S'MORES TRUFFLE
S'MORES CARAMEL BARK
S'MORES MARTINI

S'MORES MARTINI

YIELDS ONE FULL SHAKER, 5 5-OUNCE MARTINIS, OR
10 MINI MARTINIS

6 OUNCES DARK CHOCOLATE
CRUSHED GRAHAM CRACKERS AS NEEDED, FOR GARNISH
1/2 CUP CHOCOLATE VODKA
1/2 CUP BAILEYS IRISH CREAM
1/2 CUP CRÈME DE CACAO
1/2 CUP VANILLA VODKA
1 CUP HEAVY CREAM
10 LARGE MARSHMALLOWS
ICE, AS NEEDED

1. Chill martini glasses in a freezer.
2. Melt the chocolate in the top of a double boiler over low heat.
3. Dip the rim of each frozen glass in the chocolate and then into the crushed graham crackers.
4. Pour all of the remaining ingredients except the marshmallows into a martini shaker filled with ice and shake until well blended. Pour into the prepared glasses.
5. Garnish the rim with a marshmallow and then toast or light it on fire with a torch; serve immediately.

HOMEMADE MARSHMALLOWS

1/3 CUP CORNSTARCH
1/3 CUP SIFTED POWDERED SUGAR
2 CUPS GRANULATED SUGAR
1 TABLESPOON LIGHT CORN SYRUP
1 1/2 CUPS WATER
1 TEASPOON VANILLA EXTRACT
4 TABLESPOONS UNFLAVORED POWDERED GELATIN
2 EGG WHITES, ROOM TEMPERATURE

1. Combine the cornstarch and powdered sugar in a small bowl.
2. Prepare a 9-by-13-inch pan by lining it with foil so that there is some excess hanging over the sides. (This will provide ease in removing the marshmallow in following steps.) Spray the foil with nonstick cooking spray.
3. Generously sprinkle the cornstarch/sugar mixture over the entire pan. Set aside.
4. In a large pot, combine the sugar, corn syrup, and 3/4 cup of the water and then place over medium heat. Stir until the sugar is completely dissolved and then stop stirring, allowing the mixture to come to a boil.
5. Continue boiling until it reaches 260 degrees on a candy thermometer (hard-ball stage). (This process takes awhile, so prepare the gelatin and beat the egg whites in the subsequent steps while the sugar syrup cooks, keeping a close eye on the sugar syrup so that it does not go above 260 degrees.)
6. While the sugar syrup cooks, prepare the gelatin mixture. In a small saucepan, combine the remaining 3/4 cup water and the vanilla extract.
7. Sprinkle the gelatin over the top and stir briefly. Let the gelatin sit until it is completely absorbed by the liquid (about 5 minutes).
8. Set the pan over low heat and stir constantly until the mixture is liquefied.
9. While the sugar syrup cooks and the gelatin is softening, place the room-temperature egg whites in the clean bowl of a large stand mixer fitted with the whisk attachment. Once the sugar syrup nears 245 degrees, begin to beat the egg whites. Beat them until they hold firm peaks, but do not overbeat or they will be crumbly. If the egg whites are ready before the sugar syrup reaches the correct temperature, stop the mixer until the sugar syrup is ready.
10. Whisk the gelatin mixture into the sugar syrup. This mixture now needs to be poured into the egg whites. If your saucepan has a spout, pour it from the saucepan, but if it does not, I recommend pouring the syrup into a large measuring cup or pitcher so that it is easier to pour. The sugar syrup is very hot and can cause painful burns if it accidentally spills or splatters. With the mixer running on low, carefully pour the hot syrup in a thin stream into the egg whites.
11. Once all of the sugar syrup is poured, turn the mixer to

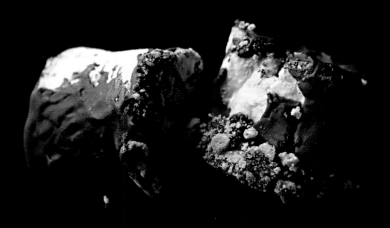

medium-high. Continue to beat the marshmallow in the mixer until it is thick enough to hold its shape and is completely opaque. (Depending on your mixer, this will take about 5-10 minutes.)

12. Pour the marshmallow mixture into the prepared 9-by-13-inch pan and smooth the top flat with an offset spatula. Let the marshmallow sit at room temperature for several hours or overnight to fully set.

13. Once the marshmallow has set, dust your work surface with a generous layer of the sugar/starch mixture you used to prepare the pan.

14. Lift the marshmallow from the pan using the foil as handles, and then flip it facedown on the prepared surface. Peel the foil off the top of the marshmallow, and dust the top of the candy with more sugar/starch.

15. Spray a large, sharp chef's knife with nonstick cooking spray. Cut the marshmallow block into small 1-inch squares, or whatever size marshmallows you desire. You can also use sharp metal cookie cutters to cut different shapes out of the marshmallow.

16. Dredge the cut edges of the marshmallows in the sugar/starch mixture so that they are not sticky. Your marshmallows are now ready to eat! They are best soon after they are made, but if your environment is not too humid, you can store them up to a week in an airtight container at room temperature. You may need to dredge the sides in sugar/starch again if they get too sticky.

ASSEMBLY: Choose a canvas plate that offers ample room for plating at least the truffle and the s'mores bark. If there is room for the martini, then plate all 3 in a row or just serve the martini alongside. For the fullest experience, serve this outside near a crackling fire. I often serve the dish accompanied by smoldering leaves in the center of the table for diners to enjoy the classic autumn aroma.

*The stroopwafel is a thin cookie made with 2 wafers and a caramel filling. In the Netherlands, it's most often eaten with a morning cup of coffee.

**The vaccination method maybe one of the easier methods because you are introducing room temperature chocolate into warm melted chocolate. This is great for keeping chocolate from getting too hot. Tempering chocolate is imperative if you want to end up with a piece of candy that doesn't melt onto your fingers while you are eating it.

CHEF OLIVER AND COMPANY SET THE STAGE.

WINE
PORT. With intense notes of deep dark fruits, raisins, and prunes, these wines are typically fortified with a neutral spirit such as brandy. A chocolate port, such as Choc-O-Block, which is essentially a fortified Tootsie roll, is a wonderful pairing.

BEER
STOUT. Stouts are dark black in color, with bold notes of coffee, chocolate, toasted nut, and a roasted-malt profile. A dry Irish stout or oatmeal stout with a modest ABV would be a great match.

extraordinary

SOME INGREDIENTS START OFF AS EXTRAORDINARY.
OTHERS BECOME EXTRAORDINARY WHEN THEY ARE PROPERLY
PREPARED. THE RECIPES IN THIS CHAPTER HIGHLIGHT BOTH.

IN MANY OF THESE RECIPES, "EXTRAORDINARY" REFERS simply to ingredients that are anything but run-of-the-mill, things you probably don't use in your everyday cooking. Foie gras, truffles, and Wagyu beef certainly fall into this category, and you will find all of those here. When using elements such as these in a recipe, my goal is to make sure that the preparation is appropriate to the ingredient: They are already at a high level, and the execution should keep them there.

In some of the recipes, however, "extraordinary" refers to dishes that take the simplest of ingredients and bring them up to a whole new level. The Slow-Braised Short Ribs are a prime example. Short ribs start out as a tough, inexpensive cut of beef, but after putting them through the process described in the recipe they are fall-apart tender. I've had diners who, after trying this dish, tell me they prefer the $4-a-pound ribs to $30-a-pound filet mignon. You might too, after you know how to make them. In this recipe, as in many others in the chapter, I hope to prove that time, effort, and patience pay big dividends.

"i hope
to prove
that time,
effort, and
patience
pay big
dividends."

foie gras

APPLE ROSEMARY PUREE, BLACK PEPPER CROSTINI, ARMAGNAC DUCK JUS

SERVES 8

FOIE GRAS CAN BE A TURN-OFF TO SOME PEOPLE.
Some consider it a taboo ingredient, and it has generated a
lot of differing opinions and political scrutiny. Whatever the
case, there is no doubt in my mind that it is an extraordinary ingredient and, when prepared correctly, it is
absolutely fabulous.

APPLE ROSEMARY PUREE

4 HONEYCRISP APPLES, PEELED, CORED, AND
   ROUGHLY CHOPPED
2 SPRIGS ROSEMARY
2 CUPS MERLOT
1 CUP LIGHTLY PACKED BROWN SUGAR
KOSHER SALT, TO TASTE
GROUND BLACK PEPPER, TO TASTE

1. In a large saucepan over low heat, simmer the apples,
rosemary, and merlot for 15 minutes.
2. Remove the rosemary sprigs and add the brown sugar.
3. Simmer until the apples are very soft.
4. Puree in a food processor to a thick applesauce consistency
and adjust the flavor to taste with salt and pepper.

ARMAGNAC DUCK JUS

1 1/4 CUPS DUCK STOCK*
1/4 CUP ARMAGNAC
KOSHER SALT, TO TASTE
GROUND BLACK PEPPER, TO TASTE

1. In a small saucepan, reduce the duck stock over medium-low
heat to one fourth of its volume.
2. Add the Armagnac and allow the alcohol to burn off (about
20 seconds).
3. Continue to reduce until the sauce has substantial body to a
nappe consistency.**

BLACK PEPPER CROSTINI

4 PIECES 8-INCH FLOUR TORTILLA OR
   LAVOSH CRACKER BREAD
2 TABLESPOONS OLIVE OIL
1 EGG WHITE, BEATEN
2 TABLESPOONS CRACKED PEPPERCORNS
1 TEASPOON KOSHER SALT

1. Preheat oven to 350 degrees.
2. Brush the flatbread with olive oil and bake on sheet pan in
the oven until they begin to crisp and turn golden.
3. Remove from the oven and brush with the egg white.
4. Sprinkle generously with the pepper and salt, then finish
cooking in the oven until the crostini are crisp and golden brown.
5. Cool and store in an airtight container.

FOIE GRAS

8 OUNCES FOIE GRAS
KOSHER SALT, TO TASTE

1. Portion the foie into 1-ounce slices approximately 1/2-inch thick.
2. Preheat saute pan over medium-high heat.
3. Sear the pieces to a deep golden brown on both sides
(about 30 seconds per side).
4. Using a spoon, baste the foie pieces with the rendered hot
fat for 30 seconds.
5. Season to taste with salt and serve immediately.

ASSEMBLY: This dish is very simple yet terrific, especially if
you like foie gras. Spoon the Apple Rosemary Puree onto the
center of the plate. Lay down a couple small chards of broken
Black Pepper Crostini. Finish with the foie, right on top, and
drizzle with the duck jus.

*You can also use 60% chicken stock and 40% beef stock if
there is no duck stock available.

**The term "nappe" refers to the ability of a liquid to coat the
back of a spoon.

WINE
SAUTERNES. Affected by the
Noble rot, these raisined grapes
have a concentrated sugar content
that renders sweet dessert wines,
which display fragrant aromas of
orange blossom and honey and
produce sweet notes of peach,
apricot, and nectarine.

CIDER
HARD APPLE CIDER. The preferred
variety to use with this dish is JK
Scrumpy Cider from Michigan,
which is crisp, refreshing, and reminiscent of orchard cider. It provides
balance to the rich foie.

trio of sliders

AMERICAN WAGYU BEEF, IOWA MAYTAG BLUE CHEESE, PAN FRIED MOREL MUSHROOMS
ANDOUILLE SAUSAGE, FRIED OYSTERS, CAJUN REMOULADE
THAI CHICKEN, KIMCHEE SLAW, RED CHILI AIOLI, BABY PEA SHOOTS
SERVES 10

1

AMERICAN WAGYU BEEF, IOWA MAYTAG BLUE CHEESE, PAN FRIED MOREL MUSHROOMS

RED ONION MARMALADE

3 TABLESPOONS UNSALTED BUTTER
6 CUPS THINLY JULIENNED RED ONIONS
   (ABOUT 3 1/4 POUNDS)
1 CUP PACKED DARK BROWN SUGAR
1/4 CUP RED WINE VINEGAR
1 CUP RED WINE
1/2 CUP DRY SHERRY
KOSHER SALT, TO TASTE
FINELY GROUND BLACK PEPPER, TO TASTE

1. Melt the butter in a large, heavy pot over medium heat.
2. Add the onions and cook until they are tender, stirring occasionally (about 30 minutes).
3. Add the brown sugar, vinegar, and red wine.
4. Cook uncovered until the onions are very tender and the mixture is thick, stirring frequently (about 20 minutes).
5. Add the sherry and continue cooking until the mixture is very thick and dark, stirring frequently.
6. Season to taste with salt and pepper and cool completely. Cover and refrigerate (can be prepared 4 days ahead).

PAN FRIED MORELS

3/4 CUP ALL-PURPOSE FLOUR
KOSHER SALT, TO TASTE
GROUND BLACK PEPPER, TO TASTE
5 TABLESPOONS UNSALTED BUTTER
20 LARGE FRESH MOREL MUSHROOMS

1. Season the flour generously with salt and pepper.
2. Heat the butter in a large skillet to medium-high heat.
3. Dredge the mushrooms one at a time in the flour mixture and knock off any excess flour.
4. Saute the mushrooms in the butter, rotating them as necessary to achieve even browning and a crispy texture (about 1 minute per side).

1.

AMERICAN WAGYU BURGER

2 POUNDS GROUND WAGYU BEEF
KOSHER SALT, TO TASTE
FRESH GROUND PEPPER, TO TASTE
10 SLIDER ROLLS (SMALL ITALIAN ROLLS)
10 OUNCES MAYTAG DAIRY FARMS BLUE CHEESE
3 OUNCES BABY ARUGULA, TO GARNISH

1. Preheat grill to high heat.
2. Form the ground Wagyu into small burgers (2-3 ounces each) and season them to taste with salt and pepper.
3. Grill the burgers to your preferred doneness and then remove from the grill.
4. Warm the slider rolls on the grill.
5. Slice or crumble Maytag cheese to top each burger.
6. Garnish with the arugula, panfried morels, and red onion marmalade.

2.

3.

trio of sliders

AMERICAN WAGYU BEEF, IOWA MAYTAG BLUE CHEESE, PAN FRIED MOREL MUSHROOMS
ANDOUILLE SAUSAGE, FRIED OYSTERS, CAJUN REMOULADE
THAI CHICKEN, KIMCHEE SLAW, RED CHILI AIOLI, BABY PEA SHOOTS

2
ANDOUILLE SAUSAGE, FRIED OYSTERS, CAJUN REMOULADE

ANDOUILLE SAUSAGE*

1 TEASPOON POWDERED CAYENNE PEPPER, OR TO TASTE**
1/2 TABLESPOON PAPRIKA
2 TABLESPOONS CHOPPED FRESH GARLIC
1 TABLESPOON FRESHLY GROUND BLACK PEPPER
1 1/2 TABLESPOONS KOSHER SALT
1/2 TABLESPOON CHOPPED FRESH THYME LEAVES
1/2 TEASPOON CRUSHED RED PEPPER
1/4 CUP ICE WATER
2 1/2 POUNDS PORK (BOSTON BUTT), TRIMMED OF TOUGH CONNECTIVE TISSUE AND CUT INTO 2-INCH CUBES

1. Combine all of the sausage ingredients except for the pork in a large mixing bowl.
2. Add the pork to the bowl and mix it with the seasonings, making sure it is well coated.
3. Cover tightly with plastic wrap and refrigerate for 1-2 days.
4. Grind the meat mixture with a coarse grinding plate. For burgers, this is all that is needed.
5. Pat the ground sausage into 3-ounce portions and then sear the burgers in a skillet preheated over medium-high heat or on a grill over medium heat. Keep warm for service.

FRIED OYSTERS

CANOLA OIL, FOR DEEP-FRYING
1 TEASPOON SEA SALT
1/2 TEASPOON GROUND BLACK PEPPER
1 CUP ALL-PURPOSE FLOUR
20 STANDARD-COUNT OYSTERS, SHUCKED

1. Pour the canola oil into a 6-quart pot over moderate heat to about 2 inches deep.
2. Bring the oil temperature to 350 degrees.
3. Combine the salt, pepper and flour in a mixing bowl.
4. Dredge the oysters a few at a time into the flour mixture, patting off the excess; deep-fry the oysters in the oil until they are crispy on the outside (about 2 minutes).
5. Remove the oysters from the oil to a paper towel-lined pan.
6. Repeat the process for the remaining oysters.

CAJUN REMOULADE

YIELDS 2 CUPS

3 EGG YOLKS
1/3 CUP VEGETABLE OIL
1/4 CUP CHOPPED GREEN ONION
1/8 CUP FRESH PARSLEY
2 TABLESPOONS DIJON MUSTARD
1 TABLESPOON WORCESTERSHIRE SAUCE
1 TABLESPOON CHAMPAGNE VINEGAR
1 TABLESPOON TABASCO SAUCE
1 TABLESPOON MINCED GARLIC
2 TABLESPOONS LEMON JUICE
1 TABLESPOON KETCHUP
1 TEASPOON BLACK MAGIC CAJUN SPICE
KOSHER SALT, TO TASTE
10 SLIDER ROLLS (SMALL ITALIAN ROLLS)

1. In a food processor, beat the egg yolks and then stream in the oil while the machine is running.
2. Blend in all of the remaining ingredients (except buns) until well blended.
3. Adjust seasoning to taste with salt.

3
THAI CHICKEN, KIMCHEE SLAW, RED CHILI AIOLI, BABY PEA SHOOTS

KIMCHEE SLAW

1 ENGLISH CUCUMBER, JULIENNED†
1 CUP SHREDDED RADICCHIO
2 CUPS SHREDDED NAPA CABBAGE
1 TABLESPOON SOY SAUCE
2 TABLESPOONS SRIRACHA CHILI SAUCE
1 TABLESPOON SESAME OIL

1. Combine all of the slaw ingredients and allow the flavors to marry at least 1 hour before serving.

RED CHILI AIOLI

1 CUP MAYONNAISE
2 WHOLE DRIED RED CHILIS, REHYDRATED‡
1 TEASPOON LIME ZEST
1/2 TEASPOON LIME JUICE

1. Using a stick blender or food processor, blend all of the red chili aioli ingredients until smooth.

CHICKEN BURGER

2 POUNDS GROUND CHICKEN
2 TABLESPOONS CANOLA OIL
TABLESPOON THAI CHILI PASTE
TABLESPOON CHOPPED CILANTRO
2 TABLESPOONS SOY SAUCE
TABLESPOON SESAME OIL
KOSHER SALT, TO TASTE
GROUND BLACK PEPPER, TO TASTE
0 SLIDER ROLLS (SMALL ITALIAN ROLLS)
OUNCE BABY PEA SHOOTS, TO GARNISH

. Blend all of the burger ingredients and form into small
burgers (2-3 ounces each).
2. Preheat skillet over medium-high heat.
3. Sear the chicken burgers in oil on both sides until golden
brown (about 2 minutes per side).
4. Turn down the heat to medium and continue cooking the
burgers to 160 degrees internal temperature.
5. Warm the slider rolls in a 325-degree oven for
minutes.

SEMBLY: These little sliders can be served up as a trio tasting,
as a tapas-style offering, or individually as dinner for the family.
Add some chips or potato salad and you are in business. As far
as the assembly of each burger, just throw the components
straight on the slider roll and you're rockin' out.

*This recipe yields more than 10 servings. Properly divide and
store extra sausage in the freezer.

**Remember, if you make the sausage too hot, every dish you
make with it will be too hot! Start off with a little of the pepper;
you can add more after you taste the finished sausages.

*To julienne the cucumber, cut it into neat 2-inch matchsticks
about 1/8-inch thick

To rehydrate dried chilis, pour boiling water over them and
let them steep until they are soft (at least 30 minutes).

WINE: **ZINFANDEL (BEEF), CHAMPAGNE (SAUSAGE), SAUVIGNON BLANC (CHICKEN).** Sweet and jammy, with a luscio
blackberry pie, vanilla, pepper spice and cigar boxes, zinfandels have a full-bodied mouth-feel and are quite versatile with red
preferred choice of champagne is blanc de noir, which is highly carbonated, with notes of wild strawberry, hay, dried fruits, bi
Sauvignon blanc is crisp and refreshing, with racy acidity and a clean, dry finish, and displays fresh notes of floral and herbal
with ripe melon and tropical fruits on the palate.

BEER: **DUBBEL (BEEF), SCHWARZBIER (SAUSAGE), INDIA PALE ALE (CHICKEN).** Malty and complex, dubbels display r
dark fruit, and spice. Schwarzbier is a German-style lager that displays bready notes on the nose and bitter chocolate with a d
Highly hop-forward with an intense, full-flavored mouth feel of orange and grapefruit citrus, with fragrant, floral notes on the
contrast to spicy notes in any dish.

slow-braised short ribs
RAMELIZED PEARL ONIONS, HORSERADISH MASHED POTATOES,
GAUFRETTE CHIPS, RED WINE JUS
ES 10-12

ECIPE IS A PERFECT EXAMPLE OF HOW PUTTING
some extra love and patience into a dish pays dividends on
the palate. I assure you that this recipe will make you
rethink your favorite cut of meat. Step aside, filet and
porterhouse: Here come short ribs.

-BRAISED SHORT RIBS*
4 POUNDS BONELESS SHORT RIBS OR
  6 POUNDS BONE-IN SHORT RIBS
KOSHER SALT, TO TASTE
FINELY GROUND BLACK PEPPER, TO TASTE
3 CARROTS, PEELED AND ROUGHLY CHOPPED
1 ONION, ROUGHLY CHOPPED
3 RIBS CELERY, ROUGHLY CHOP (NO LEAVES)
6 CLOVES GARLIC
3 CUPS RED WINE

1. Preheat oven to 300 degrees.
2. Preheat a roasting pan over medium-high heat.
3. Generously season the short ribs with kosher salt and
pepper and then sear them in the hot pan on all sides. Allow
the fat to render from the short ribs into the pan.
4. Transfer the ribs to a plate and then pan-roast the carrots,
onions, celery, and garlic in the pan drippings.
5. Remove the pan from heat and then place the seared short
ribs on top of the roasted mirepoix.**
6. Add the red wine to the ribs and vegetables. Cover and seal
the pan using aluminum foil, a tight-fitting lid, or both. (It is very
important to get a good seal before finishing the braising
technique in the oven.)
7. Place the roasting pan in the oven and braise the short ribs
until they are tender (about 4 hours).
8. When they are tender, remove the short ribs from the pan
and strain the braising liquid through a fine-mesh sieve, discarding the solids.
9. Chill the liquid. Remove and discard the fat from the top of
the chilled braising liquid. Reserve the braising liquid to use in
the red wine jus recipe that follows.

WINE: **BORDEAUX.** Robust and complex, with intense notes of tobacco, cedar, cherry jam, blackberry, and dried fruits, Bordeaux wines have a firm, tannic mouthfeel, Old World, earthy minerality, and a long finish. Be sure to decant for at least 1 to 2 hours prior to serving.

BEER: **BIÈRE DE GARDE.** Copper in color, with notes of spice and bready malt on the nose, bières de garde demonstrate flavors of anise, wood, sage, and fennel.

slow-braised short ribs
CARAMELIZED PEARL ONIONS, HORSERADISH MASHED POTATOES, GAUFRETTE CHIPS, RED WINE JUS

CARAMELIZED PEARL ONIONS

1 TABLESPOON UNSALTED BUTTER
20 PEARL ONIONS, PEELED
2 TABLESPOONS RED WINE
KOSHER SALT, TO TASTE
GROUND BLACK PEPPER, TO TASTE

1. Preheat a skillet over medium heat.
2. Add the butter and pearl onions, sauteing until they are very caramelized.
3. Deglaze the pan with the red wine, scraping up any bits stuck to the bottom of the pan. Reduce the red wine to nothing.
4. Season the onions to taste with salt and pepper.

RED WINE JUS

1 CUP RED WINE
RESERVED BRAISING LIQUID (FROM SHORT RIBS RECIPE)
4 SPRIGS THYME
KOSHER SALT, TO TASTE
GROUND BLACK PEPPER, TO TASTE

1. In a small saucepan over low heat, reduce the red wine by half.
2. Add the braising liquid and thyme and reduce by half. Season to taste with salt and pepper.
3. Strain the jus through a fine-mesh sieve and reserve for re-warming short ribs.

HORSERADISH MASHED POTATOES
MAKES 8 CUPS

3 POUNDS RUSSET POTATOES, PEELED AND QUARTERED
1/2 CUP MILK
1/4 CUP HEAVY WHIPPING CREAM
1/2 CUP UNSALTED BUTTER, CHOPPED
KOSHER SALT, TO TASTE
GROUND WHITE PEPPER, TO TASTE
1/3 CUP PREPARED HORSERADISH
1/2 CUP SOUR CREAM

1. Place the quartered potatoes in a stockpot and cover them with cold water.
2. Bring to a boil, reduce heat and simmer until the potatoes are tender (about 20 minutes).
3. Meanwhile, heat the milk and heavy cream until warm.
4. Drain the potatoes well and mash while they are still hot. (The paddle attachment on a mixer can be used to mash, but be careful not to over-whip them.)
5. Add the butter to the warm potatoes and incorporate to melt.
6. Stir the milk and cream into the potato mixture.
7. Season to taste with salt and white pepper.
8. Stir in the horseradish and sour cream.

FRIED POTATO GAUFRETTE CHIPS

4 RUSSET POTATOES (ABOUT 2 POUNDS)
ABOUT 4 CUPS CANOLA OIL, FOR DEEP-FRYING
KOSHER SALT, TO TASTE

1. Prepare a large bowl of cold water.
2. Using a French-style mandoline with a wavy blade, slice each potato into paper-thin slices, rotating the potato 90 degrees after each slice to create a waffle-style cut (about $1/16$-inch thick).
3. Transfer the slices to the cold water after they are cut and let them soak for 5 minutes.
4. Working with several pieces at a time, dry the slices with a paper towel.
5. In a 3-quart saucepan, heat the oil until a deep-fat thermometer registers 350 degrees.
6. Fry the chips until they are golden ($1\frac{1}{2}$-2 minutes), making sure the oil returns to 350 degrees before adding the next batch.
7. As they are fried, use a large slotted spoon to transfer the chips to paper towels to drain.
8. Sprinkle with salt, to taste.
9. Repeat the process until all of the chips are ready. These chips can be made a few hours ahead and kept in an airtight container.

ASSEMBLY: Depending on your canvas choice, you may want to place the mashed potatoes near the center and pull them just a bit in one or two directions. The short rib meat can be placed around the plate, but be sure to pull it just a bit with a fork to create an easy dining experience. Drizzle or spoon the red wine jus on and around the meat and finish the dish with the gaufrette chips and caramelized pearl onions. This dish has it all, both in flavor as well as texture.

*The short ribs can be prepared one day in advance and re-warmed before service.

**The term "mirepoix" refers to a combination of chopped aromatic vegetables, usually two parts onion, one part carrot, and one part celery.

truffle-seared organic chicken

GNOCCHI GALETTE, CELERY ROOT PUREE, SAGE BROWN BUTTER

SERVES 8

TRUFFLE-SEARED ORGANIC CHICKEN

1 SMALL BLACK TRUFFLE, THINLY SLICED
3 10- TO 12-OUNCE BONELESS, SKIN-ON CHICKEN
   BREASTS, FRENCHED*
KOSHER SALT, TO TASTE
GROUND BLACK PEPPER, TO TASTE
1 TABLESPOON OLIVE OIL
1 TEASPOON WHITE TRUFFLE OIL

1. Place the truffle slices underneath the chicken skin.
2. Season the chicken breast to taste with salt and pepper.
3. In a hot, nonstick saute pan, drizzle the olive oil and place the breast skin side down. Saute over medium heat until it is golden brown; flip over and finish cooking in the oven (transferring to a baking pan if your saute pan isn't oven-safe) until it is cooked through (about 10 minutes).
4. Drizzle the truffle oil over the chicken breast. Let the chicken rest before slicing.

GNOCCHI GALETTE

1 3/4-2 POUNDS RUSSET POTATOES (ABOUT 5 MEDIUM-SIZE
   POTATOES), PEELED AND CUT INTO 1/2-INCH CUBES
1/2 CUP FRESHLY GRATED PARMESAN CHEESE
1 1/2 TEASPOONS KOSHER SALT
1/4 TEASPOON GROUND BLACK PEPPER
1/4 TEASPOON GROUND NUTMEG
1 LARGE EGG YOLK
1 CUP ALL-PURPOSE FLOUR, PLUS MORE AS NEEDED
10 TABLESPOONS (1 1/4 STICKS) UNSALTED BUTTER, DIVIDED
1/3 CUP THINLY SLICED FRESH SAGE

1. Bring water to a boil in the bottom of a steamer pot.
2. Steam the potatoes in a steamer basket until tender (about 15 minutes).
3. Transfer to a large bowl. Allow the potatoes to cool slightly (about 10 minutes) and then mash them until they are smooth.
4. Mix in the next 4 ingredients (Parmesan cheese, salt, pepper, and nutmeg).
5. Add the yolk and mix until blended. Gradually mix in 1 cup of the flour. Knead until blended and smooth (about 5 minutes), adding more flour by the tablespoon if the dough is very moist.
6. Line a rimmed baking sheet with parchment paper.
7. Divide the dough into 4 equal pieces. Roll 1 piece at a time on a lightly floured surface approximately 1/2-inch thick.
8. Using a circle cutter, cut the dough into galettes 2 1/2-3 inches in diameter.
9. Working in batches, cook the gnocchi in a large pot of boiling salted water until they float, then cook for 1 minute longer.
10. Using a slotted spoon, transfer the gnocchi to a towel and pat dry.
11. In saute pan, over medium-low heat, melt 2 tablespoons of unsalted butter and saute the gnocchi until they are golden brown on both sides. Serve immediately.

CELERY ROOT PUREE

3 CUPS WHOLE MILK
3 CUPS WATER
1 TABLESPOON KOSHER SALT, PLUS MORE TO TASTE
2 LARGE CELERY ROOTS (ABOUT 2 1/2 POUNDS TOTAL),
   PEELED AND CUT INTO 2-INCH CUBES
1 MEDIUM-SIZE RUSSET POTATO (ABOUT 10 OUNCES),
   PEELED AND CUT INTO 2-INCH CUBES
1 SMALL ONION, PEELED AND QUARTERED
5 TABLESPOONS UNSALTED BUTTER, CUT INTO 5 PIECES
GROUND WHITE PEPPER, TO TASTE

1. Bring the milk, water, and salt to just a boil in a large, heavy saucepan over high heat.
2. Add the celery root, potato, and onion; bring to a boil.
3. Reduce the heat to medium and simmer until the vegetables are tender (about 20 minutes).
4. Drain, discarding the cooking liquid.
5. Puree the vegetables and butter in a food processor until they are smooth.
6. Season to taste with salt and white pepper.

SAGE BROWN BUTTER SAUCE

1/2 CUP UNSALTED BUTTER
2 TEASPOONS FRESH SAGE CHIFFONADE**
KOSHER SALT, TO TASTE
GROUND BLACK PEPPER, TO TASTE

1. In a heavy saucepan over medium heat, cook the butter until it is brown.
2. Remove from heat and strain through a fine-mesh sieve.
3. Add the sage and adjust the seasoning to taste with salt and pepper. Serve immediately.

ADDITIONAL INGREDIENTS

TRUFFLE OIL, TO GARNISH
SLICED TRUFFLE, TO GARNISH

ASSEMBLY: The celery root puree should be very light, making it workable on the plate. Start this assembly with a nice thick streak of the puree. Nestle the gnocchi galette into the celery puree and top it with the sliced, truffle-scented chicken. Finish the dish with plenty of sage brown butter, as this is the element that really brings out the earthy tones in the dish — not to mention that is a classic with gnocchi. Drizzle the chicken with truffle oil and serve immediately. Garnish with sliced truffle.

*"Frenched" is a butcher's term referring to the exposed bones of a cut of meat. The bones add more flavor and tenderness to the meat and are good for presentation purposes.

**The term "chiffonade" refers to slicing an ingredient into very thin ribbons. The cut is often associated with tender herbs.

WINE

WHITE BURGUNDY. The preferred choice is a Mersault, which will show aromas of bubble gum, almond, green apple, and toasted nut, and will have an earthy minerality on the palate with a strong vanilla presence from oak aging.

BEER

AMERICAN AMBER. Medium-bodied and, as the name suggests, amber in color, these beers are balanced between slight hops bitterness and caramelized malty flavors. Breckenridge Avalanche Amber Ale is a classic example of the style and would be a great match.

kobe tenderloin

FOIE GRAS, SLICED BLACK SUMMER TRUFFLES, PAN-ROASTED RED AND GOLDEN BEETS, CRISPY FRIED BEET STRINGS, CHIVE OIL, RED WINE BEET NECTAR

SERVES 10

THIS DISH IS MOST CERTAINLY GOING TO PLEASE ANY PALATE. There is something about spending a lot of money on ingredients that automatically places you in a position to blow people out of their chairs. However, don't get fooled into thinking that expensive ingredients cook themselves. This dish could easily be the worst experience in this cookbook if executed improperly. That being said, timing is fundamental to the success of this dish. When dealing with foie gras, you have a very small window of time from the pan — where it has been perfectly cooked — to the mouth. Knowing this and respecting the timing is half the battle in performing this tenderloin/foie combination.

PAN-ROASTED BEETS

2 RED BEETS
2 GOLDEN BEETS
¼ CUP UNSALTED BUTTER
KOSHER SALT, TO TASTE
GROUND WHITE PEPPER, TO TASTE

1. Peel and slice the beets into ¼-inch-thick pieces, reserving the peels from the red beets to use in the Red Wine Beet Nectar recipe that follows.
2. Prepare an ice water bath and set aside.
3. Keeping the red and golden beets in separate pots, cover them with cold water and bring to a simmer. Cook until they are just tender.*
4. Drain the beets (reserving the cooking liquid from the red beets to use in the Red Wine Beet Nectar) and shock them in ice water to set the texture.
5. Preheat a skillet over medium-high heat.
6. Add the butter and pan-roast the golden beet slices on both sides.
7. Remove from the pan and add the red beets, roasting until golden brown and warmed though.
8. Season the beets to taste with salt and pepper and keep warm for service.

RED WINE BEET NECTAR

1 CUP RED WINE
2 CUPS RED BEET COOKING LIQUID (FROM RECIPE AT LEFT)
PEELINGS FROM RED BEETS (FROM RECIPE AT LEFT)
½ CUP GRANULATED SUGAR
KOSHER SALT, TO TASTE
GROUND WHITE PEPPER, TO TASTE

1. In a medium-size saucepan over medium heat, reduce the red wine by half its volume.
2. Add the beet cooking liquid and peelings and continue reducing to 1 cup.
3. Add the sugar and then reduce the liquid to form a glaze.**
4. Season to taste with salt and white pepper.

CRISPY FRIED BEET STRINGS

CANOLA OIL, AS NEEDED
2 RED BEETS, PEELED
2 TABLESPOONS CORNSTARCH
KOSHER SALT, TO TASTE

1. Prepare a large bowl of cold water and set it aside.
2. Preheat the oil to 330 degrees in a deep fryer or deep pot.
3. On a turning mandoline with the julienne blade, spin the beets to produce long strings. Immediately transfer to the cold water to firm them (about 30 minutes).†
4. Drain the beet strings and pat them dry with a paper towel.
5. In manageable bunches, dust the beet strings with cornstarch and then fry them in the oil until crisp.
6. Remove the strings from the oil onto a paper towel-lined pan and then season to taste with salt.

kobe tenderloin

FOIE GRAS, SLICED BLACK SUMMER TRUFFLES,
PAN-ROASTED RED AND GOLDEN BEETS, CRISPY FRIED BEET STRINGS,
CHIVE OIL, RED WINE BEET NECTAR

CHIVE OIL

4 OUNCES CHIVES
3 TABLESPOONS CANOLA OIL
KOSHER SALT, TO TASTE

1. Prepare an ice water bath and set it aside.
2. Bring a medium-size pot of water to a boil.
3. Blanch the chives in the boiling water for 10 seconds and then shock in the ice water to set the color.
4. Drain and pat the chives dry with a paper towel.
5. Blend the oil and chives in a blender or food processor until smooth. Allow to stand for at least 30 minutes.
6. Strain the oil through a fine-mesh sieve and season to taste with salt.

FOIE GRAS

5 OUNCES FOIE GRAS
KOSHER SALT, TO TASTE

1. Portion the foie gras into 1/2-ounce slices approximately 1/3-inch thick.
2. Preheat saute pan over medium-high heat.
3. Sear the pieces to a deep golden brown on both sides (about 30 seconds per side).
4. Using a spoon, baste the foie pieces with the rendered hot fat for 30 seconds.
5. Season to taste with salt and serve immediately.

KOBE TENDERLOIN

10 4-OUNCE KOBE BEEF MEDALLIONS
KOSHER SALT, TO TASTE
FRESHLY GROUND BLACK PEPPER, TO TASTE
CANOLA OIL, AS NEEDED

1. Preheat a skillet to medium-high heat.
2. Season the Kobe medallions to taste with salt and pepper.
3. Rub the pan's surface with canola oil using a paper towel.
4. Sear the medallions quickly on top, bottom, and all sides. Serve rare.

ADDITIONAL INGREDIENTS

SHAVED BLACK TRUFFLES, TO GARNISH

ASSEMBLY: Working quickly with your chosen vessel, arrange the roasted beets artfully, leaving a center spot available for the rested tenderloin. Once the tenderloin is in position, drizzle the plate with the beet nectar and chive oil. Top the filet with the foie gras that has just finished searing. Garnish the plate with the fried beet strings and shaved black truffles; serve immediately.

*Test with a knife or a cake tester to determine doneness. If you are able to slide the blade into the slices easily with no resistance, they are done.

**When a sugar reduction is hot its viscosity is very thin. A good way to test this is to chill a small plate in the refrigerator; once you think the reduction is close to the right consistency, drizzle a small amount of the syrup onto the cold plate. This will give you a good indication of the consistency of the syrup.

†A turning mandoline can be used to make long, continuous strands of a vegetable or fruit.

WINE
CABERNET SAUVIGNON. Aromas of dark red fruit, tobacco, wild game, pepper spice, and vanilla echo the palate in Cabernets, which feature broad tannins, velvety mouthfeel, and a long, silky finish. These wines are big and bold enough to hold up to the rich, velvety texture of the beef while complimenting the earthy notes of the dish.

BEER
DUBBEL. Malty and complex in character, with medium to full body and only a mild hops bitterness, these rich flavored ales of Belgium display notes of raisins, figs, dark fruit, and spice. Lively carbonation makes dubbels a good compliment to the hearty beef and rich foie gras in the dish.

E CRÈME BRÛLÉE

2 CUPS HEAVY WHIPPING CREAM
PINCH KOSHER SALT
TABLESPOONS INSTANT GROUND COFFEE
WHOLE EGGS
EGG YOLKS
½ CUP GRANULATED SUGAR
¼ CUP KAHLÚA LIQUEUR
TURBINADO SUGAR, AS NEEDED

. In a heavy saucepan over medium heat, simmer the cream, salt, and instant coffee.
2. In a mixing bowl, beat the whole eggs, egg yolks, and the sugar together.
3. Temper the egg mixture with the hot cream mixture, slowly adding the cream while whisking briskly; return the entire mixture to the saucepan.
4. Reduce heat to low and continue cooking, whisking constantly until the custard begins to thicken.
5. Add the Kahlúa and continue cooking the custard over low heat, whisking constantly, until it is thick but pourable. (It should just hold onto your fingertip when dipped into it.)
6. Remove from heat and pour the custard evenly into 4-ounce ramekins or another desired vessel.
7. Allow the custard to cool to room temperature, cover it with plastic wrap, and then store it in the refrigerator to chill t completely.
8. When you are ready to serve, coat the top of the custard with the turbinado sugar.
9. Use a kitchen torch to evenly caramelize the top of each crème brûlée.

HAZELNUT BRITTLE

YIELDS ABOUT 2 POUNDS

UNSALTED BUTTER (TO PREP BAKING SHEETS), PLUS 1 MORE TABLESPOON
5 CUPS OF YOUR FAVORITE BREWED COFFEE
1 ½ CUPS GRANULATED SUGAR
⅓ CUP LIGHT CORN SYRUP
⅓ CUP DARK CORN SYRUP
2 CUPS COARSELY CHOPPED HAZELNUTS
½ TABLESPOON BAKING SODA
½ TEASPOON KAHLÚA

1. Butter 2 18-by-15-inch heavy baking sheets.
2. In a large, heavy saucepan, reduce the coffee over medium heat until 2 cups remain.
3. Stir in the sugar and both corn syrups and then dissolve over medium heat.
4. Increase heat to high and boil without stirring until a candy thermometer registers 260 degrees (about 45 minutes).
5. Reduce heat to medium-low. Mix in the hazelnuts and the 1 tablespoon of butter and cook until the thermometer registers 295 degrees, stirring constantly (about 15 minutes).
6. Add the baking soda and Kahlúa and stir this briskly as the mixture foams up. Immediately pour the mixture onto the prepared baking sheets, dividing it evenly among them. Spread out the brittle as thinly as possible.
7. Let the mixture stand until it is cool and hard. Break the brittle into pieces and store in airtight containers.

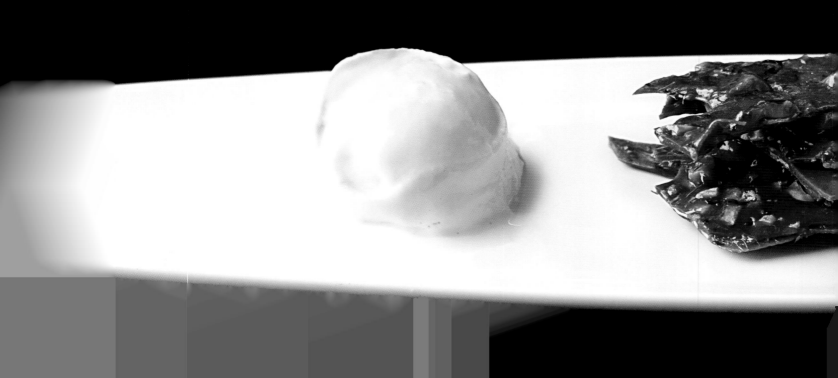

IRISH CREAM ICE CREAM

2 CUPS HEAVY WHIPPING CREAM
1 CUP HALF-AND-HALF
1 PINCH KOSHER SALT
1 TEASPOON VANILLA EXTRA
2 LARGE EGGS
1/4 CUP PACKED LIGHT BROWN SUGAR
1/2 CUP BAILEYS IRISH CREAM

1. In a 2-quart heavy saucepan over medium heat, bring the cream, half-and-half, salt, and vanilla just to a boil.
2. In a large mixing bowl, whisk together the eggs and the brown sugar.
3. Add the hot cream mixture to the egg mixture in a slow stream, whisking constantly.
4. Pour the custard into the saucepan and cook over moderately low heat, stirring constantly with a wooden spoon until it is thick enough to coat the back of the spoon and an instant-read thermometer registers 170-175 degrees (about 5 minutes); do not let the custard boil.
5. Pour the custard through a fine-mesh sieve into a bowl and then add the Baileys Irish Cream.
6. Let the custard cool completely, stirring it occasionally.
7. Cover the bowl and transfer to the refrigerator to chill completely (at least 3 hours).
8. Freeze the custard in an ice cream maker.
9. Transfer the ice cream to an airtight container and put in the freezer to harden. (Due to the Bailey's, this ice cream will have a slightly softer texture compared to other ice creams.)

ASSEMBLY: First, consider that the ice cream is soft because of the alcohol content. Also, we want to be able to plate this dish on a frozen vessel. You may opt to put the ice cream in a smaller vessel and then present that dish along with the other items. But keep in mind that the crème brûlée is going to be in its own vessel as well.

WINE
TAWNY PORT. Notes of caramel, walnut, coffee, and almond dominate the nose and palate of these fortified wines.

BEER
CHOCOLATE STOUT. Usually brewed with cocoa nibs, these stouts exude aromas of coffee, chocolate, and roasted malt while the palate echoes baker's chocolate; they have a rich, creamy mouthfeel and a bitter-sweet finish.

deconstructed

DECONSTRUCTION IS ABOUT ISOLATING INGREDIENTS FOR A PURPOSE. IT'S TAKING FAMILIAR DISHES DOWN TO THEIR ROOTS BY INDIVIDUALIZING THE CORE COMPONENTS.

IN CULINARY CIRCLES, THE TERM "DECONSTRUCTED" has been thrown around a lot. Some people might even say it's dated. But the simple fact is, there is no better way to explain the concept in one word. I like to use this approach because it allows me to exploit individual ingredients that might just fade together in the traditional preparation. Soups and salads, and especially casseroles, are typically excellent starting points for deconstructed dishes because they are made up of many ingredients all mixed together. Making a casserole involves putting everything in a pan, covering it with foil, sticking it the oven, then taking it out when it's done. But with a little more time, detail, and, most importantly, creativity, some of those timeworn casseroles can become show-stoppers. Take my Moussaka recipe. Traditionally, all the ingredients in this classic Greek casserole are cooked together, and, as a result, they all end up having a similar, soft texture. But

my version is all about separating the ingredients in order to enhance their textures. I looked at traditional moussaka and asked, "What don't I like about it?" For one thing, the eggplant is mushy, and for another, the lamb is usually overcooked. So in my recipe, the lamb is seared to medium-rare and the eggplant is floured and then pan-fried until it's crispy. After preparing each component individually, I can just stack them myself.

Ultimately, what I want you to take away from this chapter is that you can use this approach with lots of dishes you're familiar with. Once you have walked through that door, the range of possibilities is virtually endless.

"i like to use this approach because it allows me to exploit individual ingredients."

shrimp & corn chowder

GRILLED SHRIMP, ROASTED CORN, POTATO PUREE,
PEPPER BACON SPEARS, THYME CRÈME FRAÎCHE,
POTATO HERB FOSSILS

SERVES 10

POTATO PUREE

3 POUNDS YUKON GOLD POTATOES,
    PEELED AND LARGE-DICED
1 CUP MILK, SCALDED
1/2 CUP UNSALTED BUTTER
KOSHER SALT, TO TASTE
GROUND WHITE PEPPER, TO TASTE

1. Cook the potatoes in boiling water until they are tender
(about 8-10 minutes).
2. Drain and pass through a ricer.
3. Place potatoes in a medium bowl with the butter and half
the milk and then whip until smooth.
4. Place in saucepan over medium heat and whisk in the
remaining milk until the mixture has a ribbon-like consistency.
5. Season to taste with salt and pepper. Keep warm.

POTATO HERB FOSSILS

1/4 CUP UNSALTED BUTTER, MELTED
2 LARGE RUSSET POTATOES, PEELED
1 1/2 TABLESPOONS FRESH THYME LEAVES
KOSHER SALT, TO TASTE

1. Preheat oven to 250 degrees.
2. Line a large baking sheet with a Silpat baking
mat. Brush the mat with butter and season to
taste with salt.
3. Using a mandoline, cut paper-thin slices of
potatoes lengthwise and then place them on the
prepared mat. Sprinkle with thyme leaves.
4. Cover potatoes with a second mat and weigh it
down with a second baking sheet to keep it flat.
5. Bake in the oven for about 1 hour or until potatoes
are golden brown and crisp.

THYME CRÈME FRAÎCHE

2 CUPS HEAVY WHIPPING CREAM
2 TABLESPOONS BUTTERMILK
1 TEASPOON FRESH THYME LEAVES
KOSHER SALT, TO TASTE

1. Heat heavy cream to a simmer.
2. Remove from heat and incorporate buttermilk.
3. Allow mixture to ferment at room temperature until thickened
and lightly soured (approximately 8 hours or overnight).
4. Season with salt and fold in fresh thyme. Refrigerate.

PEPPER BACON SPEARS

2 SLICES BLACK PEPPER BACON

1. Lay bacon on a cutting board and slice each piece in half horizontally. Slice each half vertically into thirds. (This should give you a total of six strips out of one piece of bacon.)
2. In a skillet over medium-high heat, render the bacon until crispy. Move to a paper towel to drain.

GRILLED JUMBO SHRIMP

3 POUNDS U8 SHRIMP IN SHELL, PEELED AND DEVEINED*
3 TABLESPOONS MINCED GARLIC
3/4 TEASPOON KOSHER SALT
5 TABLESPOONS FRESH LEMON JUICE
1/2 TEASPOON GROUND BLACK PEPPER
3/4 CUP OLIVE OIL
2 TABLESPOONS FINELY CHOPPED FRESH OREGANO
1/2 CUP WHITE WINE
1 TABLESPOON CHOPPED PARSLEY
1 TABLESPOON MINCED CHIVES

1. Blend all ingredients except shrimp to make a marinade.
2. Marinade shrimp for 30 minutes.
3. Grill over medium-high heat (2 minutes on each side).

ROASTED CORN

6 LARGE EARS OF SWEET CORN, HUSKED
1/8 CUP OLIVE OIL
KOSHER SALT, TO TASTE

1. Simmer corn in boiling salted water until 1/2 tender (about 5 minutes).
2. Remove and shock in ice water. Pat ears of corn dry with a paper towel.
3. Brush with olive oil and season to taste with salt.
4. Grill over high heat rotating often, until tender and roasted (about 5 minutes).
5. Slice kernels off the cob for assembly.

ASSEMBLY: This dish is essentially a deconstructed soup, and I feel it should be presented in a large, shallow bowl. Streak the potato puree across the vessel and top the puree with two grilled shrimp. Finish with the peppered bacon and the crème fraîche, roasted corn sliced off the cob, and the thyme potato crisps. This dish could be a starter or the main attraction.

*This number indicates how the shrimp are sized during packing; in this case there are 8 shrimp per pound.

WINE
PINOT GRIS. In particular, Pinots Gris from Alsace show bright lemon-citrus aromas, an herbal spice presence, and a nice crisp acidity to refresh the palate between bites.

BEER
PILSNER. Traditional German pilsners are golden in color, with light floral hops aromas and a snappy, clean finish. Jever is a fantastic Friesland pils that would pair well.

tuna nicoise

SEARED BLUEFIN TUNA, SOFT-BOILED QUAIL EGG, MICRO GREENS, RED BLISS POTATO, HARICOT VERT PUREE, LEMON ANCHOVY VINAIGRETTE, NICOISE OLIVES, AGED BALSAMIC

SERVES 10

SALADS WORK PARTICULARLY WELL IN THE DECONSTRUCTED concept. Traditionally, this French salad, in the style of Nice, includes haricots verts, or green beans, mixed with other ingredients. I decided to isolate the varied ingredients that often appear in a Nicoise salad and use them in a nontraditional way. So, for example, instead of pan-roasting the green beans, I've provided instructions for making a haricot vert puree. The same elements of a Nicoise salad are here, but it's a whole different take on the dish.

tuna nicoise

SEARED BLUEFIN TUNA, SOFT-BOILED QUAIL EGG, MICRO GREENS, RED BLISS POTATO,
HARICOT VERT PUREE, LEMON ANCHOVY VINAIGRETTE, NICOISE OLIVES, AGED BALSAMIC

SEARED BLUEFIN TUNA

3 8- TO 10-OUNCE BLUEFIN TUNA STEAKS (1 1/4-INCH THICK)
SEA SALT, TO TASTE
FINELY GROUND BLACK PEPPER, TO TASTE
1 TABLESPOON CANOLA OIL

1. Preheat a medium saute pan over medium-high heat.
2. Season tuna generously with salt and pepper.
3. Add oil to the pan and sear on all sides, including edges.
Keep tuna rare – cook for only 1 minute on each side.
4. Remove tuna from heat and allow to rest for 5 minutes
before slicing.

LEMON ANCHOVY VINAIGRETTE

1/4 CUP FRESHLY SQUEEZED LEMON JUICE
1/2 TEASPOON DIJON MUSTARD
1/2 TEASPOON SEA SALT
1/4 TEASPOON GROUND BLACK PEPPER
3/4 CUP EXTRA VIRGIN OLIVE OIL
4 ANCHOVY FILLETS
1 EGG YOLK

1. Using a stick blender, puree together the anchovy, egg yolk,
lemon juice, mustard, salt, and pepper.
2. Slowly blend in the olive oil.

HARICOT VERT PUREE

1 POUND HARICOTS VERTS, TRIMMED
3 TABLESPOONS UNSALTED BUTTER, SOFTENED
3 TABLESPOONS CHOPPED FLAT-LEAF PARSLEY
1/2 TEASPOON GRATED LEMON ZEST
1 TEASPOON FRESH LEMON JUICE
2 TABLESPOONS OLIVE OIL
KOSHER SALT, TO TASTE
FRESHLY GROUND WHITE PEPPER, TO TASTE

1. Cook beans in a pot of boiling salted water (1 tablespoon of
salt per 6 quarts of water), uncovered, until tender
(approximately 6 minutes).
2. Drain and place beans in an ice water bath to chill.
3. Remove the beans from the ice bath and drain.
4. In a food processor, add all of the ingredients and puree until
very smooth. The puree should be able to ribbon and hold its
form on the plate.*
5. Adjust seasoning to taste with salt and pepper.
6. Re-warm puree over low heat for assembly.

FOR SALAD

10 QUAIL EGGS (SOFT-BOILED, PEELED, AND QUARTERED)**

1. Cook the eggs in a small pot of boiling water for 2 minutes, 45 seconds.
2. Drain, than cool under running water until completely cold.

1 CUP SMALL-DICE AND BLANCHED RED BLISS POTATO
1/4 OUNCE MICROGREENS
12 NICOISE OLIVES
AGED BALSAMIC SYRUP

ASSEMBLY: Using a medium-size plating spoon, streak the warm haricot vert puree in a thin line across a canvas plate. Artfully lay out 5 or 6 tuna slices overlapping some of the puree. Lightly dress the red potato with the vinaigrette and scatter a few pieces onto the dish. Finish garnishing the plate with microgreens, nicoise olives, and quail eggs. Dress the dish with lemon vinaigrette and balsamic syrup. Fresh cracked pepper may be offered as well.

*"Ribbon" is a cooking term meaning that when the spoon or whisk is lifted, the batter falls slowly back onto the surface of the mixture, forming a ribbon like pattern that, after a few seconds, sinks back into the batter.

**Quail eggs can be found in Asian and international grocery stores or markets.

WINE
WHITE CÔTE DU RHONE.
Hermitage or Chateauneuf-du-Pape, which have nice acidity and firm minerality, would compliment the olives, greens, and anchovy profiles of this dish. Another pairing option would be a light Spanish rosé.

BEER
BELGIAN-STYLE WITBIER. Known as "white" beer, these wheat beers are typically spiced with orange peel and coriander and carry a spritzy, light-bodied mouthfeel with a slightly tangy finish.

moussaka

HERB-CRUSTED LAMB CHOP, PAN-ROASTED EGGPLANT, TOMATOES, POTATOES, BÉCHAMEL SAUCE, OLIVE TAPENADE, GARLIC CHIPS

THERE'S NOTHING WRONG WITH TRADITIONAL MOUSSAKA. It is delicious. The traditional preparation has all of the ingredients layered together and baked as a casserole. Here I've broken it apart in order to isolate the individual ingredients and heighten the dish into something more textural and playful.

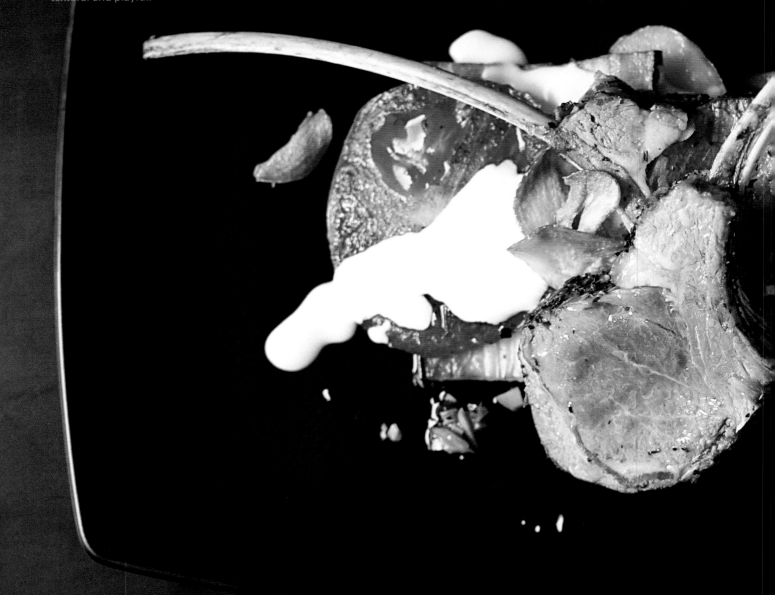

CHIANTI (CLASSICO). Medium-bodied with a firm tannic structure, Chianti Classico will show light cherry and slightly nutty and earthy mineral notes, with a very dry finish. Look for the black rooster, or "Gallo Nero" on the neck of the bottle of Classico.

BEER
BROWN ALE. Either British or American styles would work with this dish. Both will have malty backbones that feature light coffee and chocolate notes, with some caramelized malt and soft fruit notes, while American versions can have more hops bitterness. The preferred pairing is Tilburg Dutch Brown Ale from the Netherlands.

moussaka

HERB-CRUSTED LAMB CHOP, PAN-ROASTED EGGPLANT, TOMATOES, POTATOES, BÉCHAMEL SAUCE, OLIVE TAPENADE, GARLIC CHIPS

SERVES 8

LAMB

2 BUNCHES FRESH ITALIAN PARSLEY, FINELY CHOPPED
1/4 CUP FINELY CHOPPED FRESH THYME
1/4 CUP FINELY CHOPPED FRESH SAGE
1 TABLESPOON GROUND BLACK PEPPER
5 TABLESPOONS OLIVE OIL, DIVIDED
2 1 1/2-POUND, WELL-TRIMMED, 8-RIB RACKS OF LAMB, PREFERABLY FRENCHED
KOSHER SALT, TO TASTE

1. Stir fresh herbs and pepper in medium bowl to blend.
2. Add 2 tablespoons oil and mix until herbs are sticking together.
3. Firmly press 1/3 of the herb mixture over the rounded side of each rack to cover. (Can be prepared a 1 day ahead. Place on large rimmed baking sheet. Cover and refrigerate.)
4. Preheat oven to 325 degrees.
5. Heat 3 tablespoons of oil in a large nonstick skillet over medium-high heat.
6. Add 1 lamb rack to skillet, herbed side down. Sear until browned (about 3 minutes). Turn rack and sear other side (about 2 minutes).
7. Place rack, herbed side up, on rimmed baking sheet. Repeat, fitting remaining racks on same sheet; season with salt.
8. Roast lamb until thermometer inserted into center registers 125 degrees for medium-rare (about 20 minutes).
9. Let lamb rest on sheet for 5-10 minutes and cut lamb between bones into individual chops when ready to plate.

PAN-ROASTED EGGPLANT, TOMATOES, POTATOES

TOMATOES

6 EACH VINE-RIPE TOMATOES, SLICED
1 TABLESPOON FRESH OREGANO
2 TABLESPOONS OLIVE OIL
SEA SALT, TO TASTE
CRACKED BLACK PEPPER, TO TASTE

1. Preheat skillet over medium-high heat.
2. Season tomato slices with salt, pepper, and oregano.
3. Pan-roast slices in olive oil a few slices at a time, caramelizing both sides. It is important to maintain the appropriate amount of surface heat in the pan so that liquid from the tomatoes will evaporate quickly and allow the tomatoes to caramelize.

EGGPLANT

1 LARGE EGGPLANT
2 TABLESPOONS OLIVE OIL
1/2 CUP ALL-PURPOSE FLOUR
KOSHER SALT, TO TASTE
GROUND BLACK PEPPER, TO TASTE

1. Slice eggplant into 1/2-inch slices and place onto a sheet pan.
2. Salt the eggplant generously and weight with a second pan and significant additional weight. Allow the moisture to leach out for approximately 1 hour.
3. Preheat large skillet over medium heat.
4. Pat eggplant with paper towel and dust with flour.
5. Pat off excess flour and saute in olive oil until golden brown and tender.
6. Season to with salt and pepper. Keep warm for assembly.

POTATOES

3 LARGE IDAHO BAKING POTATOES, SKIN ON
3 TABLESPOONS UNSALTED BUTTER
KOSHER SALT, TO TASTE
FLESHLY GROUND WHITE PEPPER, TO TASTE

1. Start the potatoes in cold water and bring to a boil in saucepot. Reduce heat and simmer until just tender (approximately 30 minutes).
2. Remove from water and allow potatoes to cool.
3. Slice into 1/3-inch-thick slices, leaving skin on.
4. When ready to assemble, saute potato slices in butter and season to taste with salt and pepper.

BÉCHAMEL SAUCE

2 TABLESPOONS UNSALTED BUTTER
2 TABLESPOONS ALL-PURPOSE FLOUR
1 1/4 CUPS MILK, HEATED
KOSHER SALT, TO TASTE
GROUND WHITE PEPPER, TO TASTE

1. Melt the butter in a heavy-bottomed saucepan over medium heat.
2. Stir in the flour and cook, stirring constantly, until the paste cooks and bubbles a bit, but don't let it brown (about 2 minutes).
3. Add the hot milk, continuing to stir as the sauce thickens. Bring it to a boil.
4. Add salt and white pepper to taste, then lower the heat to a simmer and cook, stirring for 2-3 minutes more. Cook for a minimum of 30 minutes to a nappe consistency.*
5. Add milk as needed to prevent sauce from getting too thick.
6. Strain the sauce through a very fine sieve several times before serving.

OLIVE TAPENADE

1 CUP NICOISE OLIVES, PITTED
1 CUP PICHOLINE OLIVES, PITTED
1 TABLESPOON CAPERS
1 GARLIC CLOVE
½ TABLESPOON CHOPPED FRESH BASIL LEAVES
½ TABLESPOON CHOPPED FRESH THYME LEAVES
½ TABLESPOON CHOPPED FRESH FLAT-LEAF
    PARSLEY LEAVES
¼ TABLESPOON CHOPPED FRESH OREGANO LEAVES
¼ CUP EXTRA-VIRGIN OLIVE OIL

1. In a food processor, combine all the ingredients except the olive oil. Using the pulse button, process until coarsely chopped and well blended.
2. Continue to process, slowly adding the olive oil. Refrigerate in a covered container. Use as needed.

GARLIC CHIPS

1 LARGE GARLIC CLOVE, PEELED (USE ELEPHANT GARLIC
    IF AVAILABLE)
¼ CUP MILK
CANOLA OIL, FOR FRYING
KOSHER SALT, TO TASTE
GROUND BLACK PEPPER, TO TASTE

1. Using a mandoline, slice the garlic into ¹⁄₁₆-inch slices (very thin) and place into milk to leech out some bitterness (at least 1 hour).
2. Preheat the oil in large saucepan not more than half full to 325 degrees.
3. Remove garlic chips from milk and pat dry with a paper towel.
4. Fry in oil until crisp and golden brown (about 1 or 2 minutes). Remove from oil with slotted spoon or small strainer and season to taste with salt and pepper.

ASSEMBLY: This deconstruction brings out my favorite ingredient in traditional moussaka, which is the lamb. A Beautiful herb-roasted chop cut from a well rested rack sits atop an offering of perfectly roasted tomatoes, potatoes, and eggplant in whatever order you choose to assemble. These vegetables are dripping with a soft, neutral béchamel. The garnishes are the tapenade and the wonderful garlic chips. Great texture awaits in this dish. Choose a canvas or vessel which keeps everything tight, but allows ample room for the diner to enjoy the experience.

*The term "nappe" refers to either the ability of a liquid to coat the back of a spoon, or the act of coating a food.

whole duck
PAN-ROASTED DUCK BREAST, DUCK CONFIT RAVIOLI, BUTTERNUT SQUASH PUREE, DUCK GLACÉ

MOST WHOLE DUCK RECIPES REMIND ME OF THANKSGIVING
and are probably just that—a whole roasted duck.
However, I thought that it might be really interesting to
break the duck down and do something extremely
delicious with each part of the duck. Here for your
enjoyment is perfectly executed pan-seared duck breast
served medium-rare, succulent duck confit from the thighs
and legs transformed into delicate ravioli, and, finally,
surprising and extremely rich duck glacé from the oven-
roasted carcass. Waste not, want not!

whole duck

PAN-ROASTED DUCK BREAST, DUCK CONFIT RAVIOLI, BUTTERNUT SQUASH PUREE, DUCK GLACÉ

SERVES 8-10

WHOLE DUCK "BREAKDOWN"

This is the process for staging the entire dish.

2 WHOLE DUCKS

1. Remove legs and thighs for confit (in recipe at right).
2. Remove breast (skin-on) and reserve for pan-roasting (in recipe on opposite page).
3. Remove as much fat as possible from the remaining carcass as and use in confit recipe (at right).
4. Use remaining carcass for glacé recipe.

ROASTED DUCK GLACÉ

2 DUCK CARCASSES
1 LARGE ONION, ROUGHLY CHOPPED
2 MEDIUM CARROTS, ROUGHLY CHOPPED
2 STALKS CELERY, ROUGHLY CHOPPED
2 CLOVES GARLIC
1 BUNCH PARSLEY
3 SPRIGS THYME
2 BAY LEAVES
6 PEPPERCORNS
2 CUPS RED WINE
KOSHER SALT, TO TASTE

1. Preheat oven to 400 degrees.
2. In the oven, roast duck carcasses with onion, carrot, celery, and garlic until well browned (about 1 hour).
3. Transfer to a large stockpot and add cold water to cover by about 2 inches, then slowly bring to a boil; with a ladle, skim all of the froth from the surface as it forms.
4. Lower the heat to a simmer and add all of the remaining ingredients except for the wine.
5. Simmer, uncovered, for 3 hours.
6. Strain the stock into a large bowl through a colander lined with a double layer of dampened cheesecloth.
7. Gently press the solids to extract as much of the liquid as possible. Discard the solids and cool the liquid to room temperature. Refrigerate until chilled and lift off the solid fat that forms on the surface. Reserve the fat to be used for the confit.
8. In a large stockpot, reduce the red wine by half its volume over medium-high heat.
9. Add the cold duck stock and continue reducing to 3 cups volume. Adjust flavor to taste with salt.

DUCK CONFIT

2 TABLESPOONS KOSHER SALT
4 CLOVES GARLIC, SMASHED
8 SPRIGS THYME
COARSELY GROUND BLACK PEPPER, TO TASTE
4 DUCK LEGS AND THIGHS
ABOUT 4 CUPS DUCK FAT

1. Sprinkle half of the salt into the bottom of a dish or plastic container large enough to hold the duck pieces in a single layer.
2. Evenly scatter half of the garlic and thyme in the container.
3. Arrange the duck, skin side up, over the salt mixture, then sprinkle with the remaining salt, garlic, thyme, and a little pepper. Cover and refrigerate for 1-2 days.
4. Preheat the oven to 180 degrees.
5. Melt the duck fat in a small saucepan.
6. Brush the salt and seasonings off the duck.
7. Arrange the duck pieces in a single snug layer in a high-sided baking dish or oven-proof sauce pan.
8. Pour the melted fat over the duck (the duck pieces should be covered by the fat) and place the confit in the oven. It will just occasionally bubble; cook until the duck is tender and can be easily pulled from the bone (approximately 4 hours).
9. Remove the confit from the oven.
10. Remove the bones and strain out the duck fat. Shred the meat while it is warm. Store in the fat, if desired. Keep in the refrigerator.

PASTA DOUGH

1/2 CUP CAKE FLOUR (NOT SELF-RISING)
3/4 CUP ALL-PURPOSE FLOUR
1/2 TEASPOON KOSHER SALT
2 LARGE EGG YOLKS
1 1/2 TABLESPOONS OLIVE OIL
1/4 CUP WATER

1. Blend together all of the ingredients in a food processor until mixture begins to form a ball.
2. Knead dough on a lightly floured surface until it is smooth and elastic, incorporating only as much additional flour as necessary to keep dough from sticking (6-8 minutes).
3. Wrap dough in plastic wrap and let stand at room temperature for 1 hour.

WINE
PINOT NOIR. A medium-bodied Pinot that shows lush, jammy, red fruit notes and a tart, slightly tannic finish will be a perfect pairing for the duck. I prefer Pinots from the Willamette Valley in Oregon.

BEER
GERMAN WEISBOCK. This full-bodied dark German wheat beer is malty and has toffee and darker fruit notes such as raisin and fig. Dominant clove spice notes will be an interesting compliment to the Butternut Squash Puree.

DUCK CONFIT RAVIOLI

MAKES 16-20 RAVIOLI

2 WHOLE EGGS
1/4 CUP WATER
PASTA DOUGH (FROM RECIPE ON OPPOSITE PAGE)
DUCK CONFIT (FROM RECIPE ON OPPOSITE PAGE)
1 TEASPOON FINELY CHOPPED FRESH THYME LEAVES
1 TEASPOON FINELY CHOPPED FLAT-LEAF PARSLEY
1/4 CUP MASCARPONE CHEESE

1. Mix the confit, thyme, parsley, and mascarpone cheese in a bowl until well incorporated.
2. Beat eggs and water together in a small bowl to form an egg wash.
3. Roll out pasta dough using a thin setting on a pasta machine (to about 1/16-inch thickness).
4. Place 1 tablespoon of the confit mixture at 2-inch intervals across the dough.
5. Roll out the other half of the dough, brush it with egg wash, and press it to the first side, pressing all around the filling to make sure that it adheres.
6. Cut out the raviolis with a 2 inch circle cutter, and make sure all edges are firmly sealed.
7. Bring a large quantity of salted water to a boil and then add the ravioli. Cook until tender (about 5 minutes). Drain and keep warm for assembly.

PAN-ROASTED DUCK BREAST

4 DUCK BREASTS, SKIN ON
KOSHER SALT, TO TASTE
FRESH GROUND PEPPER, TO TASTE

1. Preheat oven to 250 degrees.
2. Preheat a large skillet over medium-low heat.
3. Season the duck breast well with salt and pepper and place skin side down in the skillet. Render the fat for about 5 minutes or until skin is very crisp.
4. Increase the heat to medium and turn the duck breast to sear the underside.
5. Place entire pan in the oven.
6. Remove the duck breast when it reaches 125 degrees internal temperature (about 5-7 minutes). Allow to rest on a cutting surface for at least 5 minutes before slicing or serving.

BUTTERNUT SQUASH PUREE

3 POUNDS BUTTERNUT SQUASH (PEELED, SEEDED, AND CUT INTO 1-INCH CUBES)
CHICKEN STOCK, AS NEEDED
3 TABLESPOONS UNSALTED BUTTER, CUT INTO PIECES
2 TABLESPOONS PURE MAPLE SYRUP
KOSHER SALT, TO TASTE
GROUND WHITE PEPPER, TO TASTE

1. Place the squash in a stockpot and cover with chicken stock. Simmer over medium heat until squash is tender. (about 15-20 minutes)
2. Strain the squash, reserving 1 cup of the liquid.
3. In a food processor or large blender, puree the squash with the butter, maple syrup, and enough of the reserved cooking liquid to reach ribbon consistency.*
4. Season the puree to taste with salt and white pepper. Keep warm for service.

ASSEMBLY: This dish deserves a nice large pasta bowl. We are looking for a bowl that has a lot of surface as well. Streak the Butternut Squash Puree across the center of the vessel using a large spoon. Slice the rested duck breast into 1/4-inch-thick pieces. Fan 4 or 5 duck slices out to one side of the puree and place 2-3 raviolis along the opposite side of the puree. It is a nice touch to jump the raviolis in a small amount of the duck glacé before plating them. Finish the dish with an ample drizzle of the glacé.

*"Ribbon" is a cooking term meaning that when the spoon or whisk is lifted, the batter falls slowly back onto the surface of the mixture, forming a ribbon like pattern that, after a few seconds, sinks back into the batter.

veal wellington

PAN-SEARED VEAL TENDERLOIN, SAUTEED ASPARAGUS & MORELS, PUFF PASTRY CRACKER, MUSHROOM DUXELLE, ROASTED BONE MARROW, GLACÉ DE VEAU

WHILE TAKING CLASSES IN FRENCH CLASSICAL CUISINE AT culinary school, I thoroughly enjoyed the classic approach to traditional Wellington. However, applying the deconstruction method and isolating the ingredients has its rewards. You be the judge.

veal wellington

PAN-SEARED VEAL TENDERLOIN, SAUTEED ASPARAGUS & MORELS, PUFF PASTRY CRACKER, MUSHROOM DUXELLE, ROASTED BONE MARROW, GLACÉ DE VEAU

SERVES 10

PUFF PASTRY CRACKER*

1 LARGE EGG
1/8 CUP WATER
2 SHEETS PUFF PASTRY (CUT INTO 1-BY-6-INCH STRIPS)
2 TABLESPOONS FINELY CHOPPED FRESH THYME
KOSHER SALT, TO TASTE
FRESHLY CRACKED BLACK PEPPER, TO TASTE

1. Preheat oven to 350 degrees.
2. Beat egg and water together to form an egg wash.
3. Using a small fork, punch holes throughout each strip of puff pastry on both sides. (Note: these holes should cover the strips of puff pastry entirely from edge to edge. This is going to keep the dough from rising during baking.)
4. Brush the prepared dough strips very lightly with egg wash and sprinkle them with thyme, salt, and pepper.
5. Bake them until golden brown (about 20-25 minutes).

SAUTEED ASPARAGUS TIPS

1 POUND ASPARAGUS TIPS (TOP 3-INCH SECTIONS ONLY)
2 TABLESPOONS UNSALTED BUTTER
2 TEASPOONS OLIVE OIL
KOSHER SALT, TO TASTE
GROUND BLACK PEPPER, TO TASTE

1. Bring 4 cups water to a boil.
2. Cook asparagus in boiling water for 1 minute or until it just starts to tender.
3. Remove from heat immediately, strain, and shock asparagus in ice water. Once chilled, strain and pat mostly dry with a paper towel.
4. Preheat a large skillet over medium heat and saute asparagus in olive oil until hot and tender, but still slightly crunchy.
5. Melt in butter and season to taste with salt and pepper. Serve immediately.

PAN FRIED MORELS

1/2 CUP ALL-PURPOSE FLOUR
KOSHER SALT, TO TASTE
GROUND BLACK PEPPER, TO TASTE
3 TABLESPOONS UNSALTED BUTTER
10 LARGE MOREL MUSHROOMS

1. Season flour generously with salt and pepper.
2. Heat butter in a large skillet to medium-high heat.
3. Dredge mushrooms one at a time in flour mixture and knock off excess flour.
4. Saute in butter and rotate mushrooms as necessary to achieve browning and crispy texture (approximately 1 minute per side).

GLACÉ DE VEAU

3 POUNDS ASSORTED VEAL BONES
1/2 CARROT, ROUGHLY CHOPPED
1 SMALL ONION, ROUGHLY CHOPPED
1 CELERY STALK, ROUGHLY CHOPPED
2 QUARTS WATER
1 BOUQUET GARNI**
1/4 CUP CHOPPED SHALLOT (ABOUT 1 SHALLOT)
2 GARLIC CLOVES, CHOPPED
1 CUP RED BURGUNDY WINE
1 TABLESPOON CANOLA OIL
KOSHER SALT, TO TASTE
GROUND BLACK PEPPER, TO TASTE

1. Preheat oven to 350 degrees.
2. Spread the bones, carrot, onion, and celery on a rimmed baking sheet.
3. Roast, tossing several times so that all of the ingredients roast evenly, until vegetables and bones have taken on deep caramel color (about 1 1/2 hours).
4. Transfer roasted vegetables and bones to a 5-quart stockpot.
5. Add 2 quarts (8 cups) water and bouquet garni and then bring to a boil. Reduce heat and simmer gently, uncovered.
6. Skim the fat off the top of the stock with a ladle to make the stock more pure.
7. Reduce until liquid measures approximately 4 cups (about 2 hours).
8. Remove and discard bones and bouquet garni.
9. Strain out vegetables and reserve liquid. Refrigerate until any remaining fat has solidified (at least 2 hours); lift off and discard the fat.
10. In a large saute pan with canola oil, warm over medium heat.
11. Add shallots and garlic and cook, stirring, until shallot is translucent.
12. Add wine and simmer until liquid is reduced by half its volume (about 10 minutes).
13. Add the veal stock and bring to boil.
14. Reduce heat and simmer until glacé measures about 1 cup (about 1 hour). Season to taste with salt and pepper.

PORTOBELLO MUSHROOM DUXELLE

- 2 TABLESPOONS UNSALTED BUTTER
- 1 TABLESPOON MINCED SHALLOT
- 16 OUNCES BABY PORTOBELLO MUSHROOMS, STEMMED AND BRUNOISE†
- ½ CUP RED WINE
- KOSHER SALT, TO TASTE
- FRESH GROUND PEPPER, TO TASTE
- 1 TABLESPOON MINCED CHIVES

1. In a stainless-steel sauteuse, melt the butter over medium-high heat and sweat the shallot for 2-3 minutes.‡
2. Add the portobello mushrooms and cook them for 5 minutes, stirring occasionally.
3. Turn heat to low and add the red wine, letting the liquid reduce completely.
4. Remove from the heat, season to taste with salt and pepper and then garnish the mixture with chives.

ROASTED BONE MARROW

- 10 VEAL SHANK BONES (2-INCH SECTIONS)

1. Preheat oven to 400 degrees.
2. Roast bones in the oven for approximately 1 hour.
3. Allow to cool to a workable temperature.
4. Using a small knife, cut around the inner cylinder of the bone to loosen the marrow. Remove the marrow in as large a piece as possible and reserve pieces for assembly.
5. Fill empty bones with mushroom duxelle and keep warm.

PAN-SEARED VEAL MEDALLIONS

- 2 POUNDS VEAL TENDERLOIN (CUT INTO 2- TO 3-OUNCE MEDALLIONS)
- ¾ CUP WONDRA FLOUR
- ¼ CUP UNSALTED BUTTER
- KOSHER SALT, TO TASTE
- COARSELY GROUND BLACK PEPPER, TO TASTE

1. Preheat a large skillet over medium-high heat.
2. Season the veal to taste with salt and pepper and then dredge in Wondra flour; pat excess flour off.
3. Working in batches, place 1 tablespoon of butter into the skillet (it will immediately melt and begin to brown). Working

quickly, sear the seasoned veal in the butter on both sides. Veal should be caramelized and removed from heat at 120 degrees. Rest veal on a sheet pan for a few minutes.

ASSEMBLY: I really like the idea of a linear presentation for this dish. There is something appealing about the traditional Wellington (layer of mushroom paste, topped with filet of beef, surrounded by puff pastry). But I like this dish broken out of its shell and laid out artfully across a plate. Let these great elements stand together and alone when you present. Stack up the seared veal, garnished with asparagus and morels, drizzled with the Glacé de Veau. Place the duxelle-filled bone next to the veal and top it with the bone marrow. Tuck the unique puff pasty cracker into it and enjoy this dish both as the diner and the creator.

*I form these crackers in various artistic ways to suit the presentation. As shown, they were baked on an inverted French loaf pan.

**To make a bouquet garni, wrap 20 parsley stems, 3 thyme sprigs, 1 teaspoon whole black peppercorns, and 2 bay leaves in an 8-inch square of cheesecloth, tying the bundle closed with kitchen twine.

†"Brunoise" refers to cutting the ingredient first into ⅛-inch matchsticks and then into ⅛-inch cubes.

‡A "sauteuse" pan is a straight-sided saute pan.

bananas foster

FRIED PLANTAIN CHIPS, VANILLA BEAN SALT, BANANA RUM ICE CREAM, 10 CANE RUM CARAMEL, DRIED BANANA CHIP BRITTLE

TRADITIONALLY, YOU MAKE BANANAS FOSTER BY SAUTEING the bananas in butter, caramelizing some brown sugar, then flaming it with rum and crème de banana and serving the whole thing with vanilla bean ice cream. But my Bananas Foster recipe is a fun and twisted version. The biggest difference is in texture. I use crunchy Plantain Chips instead of bananas, Vanilla Bean Salt, and Banana Rum Ice Cream. The recipe doesn't call for it, but you could still flambé the caramel.

bananas foster

FRIED PLANTAIN CHIPS, VANILLA BEAN SALT, BANANA RUM ICE CREAM, 10 CANE RUM CARAMEL,
DRIED BANANA CHIP BRITTLE

SERVES 12

VANILLA BEAN SALT*

1 VANILLA BEAN (SPLIT LENGTHWISE AND SCRAPED)
⅛ CUP KOSHER SALT

1. In a food processor or grinder, blend the scraped bean pulp
and salt together. Store in and airtight container.

PLANTAIN CHIPS

ABOUT 4 CUPS VEGETABLE OIL
3 GREEN PLANTAINS
VANILLA BEAN SALT, TO TASTE (SEE RECIPE ABOVE)

EQUIPMENT: Deep-fat thermometer; adjustable-blade
slicer or Y-shaped vegetable peeler.

1. Heat 1 inch of oil to 350 degrees in a
4- to 5-quart heavy pot over medium-high heat.
2. Meanwhile, cut the ends from the (unpeeled) plantains.
3. Soak the plantains in warm water to soften the peel.
4. Cut a slit lengthwise into the peel and then carefully peel the
plantain. Discard the peel.
5. Cut plantains lengthwise into very thin slices (less than $1/16$-
inch thick) with a slicer.
6. Fry plantains in batches of 3 to 4 slices. Using a couple of
pairs of small tongs, shape the plantains as they soften in the
hot oil to form tight loops. Fry until golden, turning frequently
(about 1 minute per batch).
7. Drain on paper towels, immediately seasoning each batch
lightly with vanilla bean salt. Return oil to 350 degrees
between batches.

1 1/2 CUPS HEAVY WHIPPING CREAM
1 1/2 CUPS HALF AND HALF
6 LARGE EGG YOLKS
2/3 CUP GRANULATED SUGAR
3 TABLESPOONS DARK RUM
1 POUND RIPE BANANAS (ABOUT 3 MEDIUM), PEELED
2 TABLESPOONS FRESH LEMON JUICE

1. Pour cream and half and half into heavy medium saucepan. Bring mixture to just a simmer.
2. Whisk yolks and sugar in large bowl to blend.
3. Gradually whisk hot cream mixture into the yolks to temper them.
4. Return mixture to same saucepan and stir over medium-low heat until mixture thickens and leaves a path on the back of spoon when finger is drawn across it or nappe† consistency about 7 minutes (do not boil).
5. Strain custard into clean large bowl, Stir in rum.
6. Refrigerate until cold, about 2 hours.
7. Puree bananas and lemon juice in processor until smooth.
8. Stir into custard.
9. Process in ice cream maker according to the manufacturer's instructions. Transfer to covered container and freeze. (Can be prepared 3 days ahead.)

10 CANE RUM CARAMEL

8 SERVINGS

1 1/8 CUP GRANULATED SUGAR
1/8 CUP WATER
1/4 TEASPOON LEMON JUICE
1 TABLESPOON LIGHT CORN SYRUP
3/4 CUP HEAVY WHIPPING CREAM
3 TABLESPOONS UNSALTED BUTTER
2 TABLESPOONS 10 CANE RUM (OR ANOTHER BRAND OF PURE SUGARCANE RUM)

1. Place the sugar, water, and lemon juice in a small saucepan and bring to a boil.
2. Add the corn syrup. Cook over medium heat until the syrup reaches a golden amber color.
3. Remove the pan from heat, add the heavy cream carefully. Stir with a wooden spoon to mix in the cream. If the sauce is not smooth, return the pan to the heat and cook, stirring constantly to melt any lumps.
4. Add the butter (with the pan off the heat). Keep stirring until the butter is melted and the sauce is smooth.
5. Stir in the rum.

1/4 CUP GRANULATED SUGAR
2 TABLESPOONS WATER
PINCH OF KOSHER SALT
12 DRIED BANANA CHIPS

1. Spray a large rimmed baking sheet with nonstick spray.
2. In small saucepan over medium heat, stir sugar, 2 tablespoons water, and pinch of salt until sugar dissolves. Increase heat to high. Boil without stirring until mixture turns deep amber, occasionally swirling pan and brushing down sides with wet pastry brush (about 5 minutes).
3. Remove from heat. Working quickly, coat each banana chip one at a time with the sugar and place them on the baking sheet, allowing the sugar to stream away from the chip to form a spike.
4. Cool until hardened. (Can be made 2 days ahead; store in airtight container at room temperature.)

ASSEMBLY: This dish can certainly be presented in many ways; however, the vessel I have chosen is inspired by a very simple, age-old presentation for serving onion rings on a spike or dowel. The plantain chips are literally formed into rings, which slip over the glass spike. The ice cream sits in a pool of the 10 Cane Rum Caramel. The Vanilla Bean Salt is added in a way that allows the diner to sprinkle the plantain chips as they enjoy the dish. Finish the presentation by leaning the banana chip brittle against the ice cream and serve immediately.

*Using flavored salts is a good way to enhance the taste of the item while giving it a little hint of something different.

**"Nappe" refers to the ability of a liquid to coat the back of a spoon.

WINE
MUSCAT (MOSCATO D'ASTI). Aromas of tropical fruits and musky notes echo the palate with ripe melon and mango. The light carbonation of a Moscato d'Asti leaves a refined sweetness and lifts the mouth feel with its scrubbing bubbles.

BEER
GERMAN HEFEWEIZEN. A light-bodied wheat beer, hefeweizen has a hazy, bright orange color with a nose of clove and banana that's followed by a dry and restrained bitterness, which leads to a refreshing and clean finish.

new
approach

WHEN I ORIGINALLY CONCEIVED THIS BOOK, THE recipes that are now divided into Deconstructed and New Approach were all going to be in the same chapter, because the two concepts are closely related. But the more I thought about it, I realized some of these recipes started with deconstruction then went a step further. A deconstructed French onion soup would be a broth made of caramelized onions and, instead of having a gratiné crouton, it would have a grilled cheese sandwich for dipping. But the Reverse French Onion Soup in this chapter is totally different. It is a "new approach" because, as the name suggests, it takes French onion soup and turns it around. It's a Gruyère cheese bisque served with a flat bread pizza topped with onion jam and covered with different types of onions.

The point is to encourage you to take something you've had a hundred times and, thinking creatively, do it differently. And that's why it's the last chapter. In a sense, it is the culmination of many of the concepts I have used to create the recipes throughout the book. I hope that the previous chapters have given you lots of new ideas for the way you approach cooking, and New Approach is kind of pushing you out of the nest, inspiring you to take some of those ideas and come up with your own unique versions of familiar dishes. I have supplied just five examples here, which represent my unique vision. Imagine how many other new approaches you could try on your own.

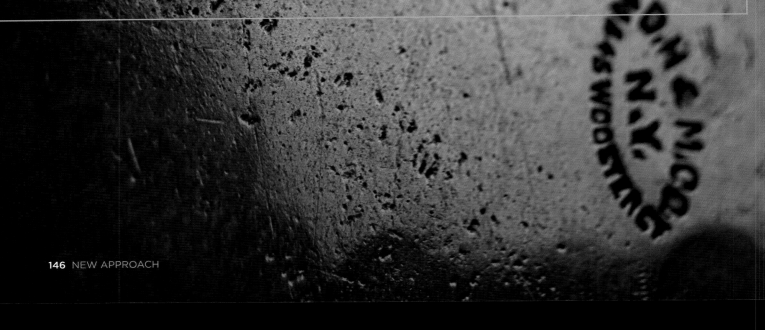

"the point is to encourage you to take something you've had a hundred times and, thinking creatively, do it differently."

reverse french onion soup

GRUYÈRE BISQUE, CARAMELIZED ONION FLATBREAD, FRIZZLED LEEKS, CHIVE OIL

SERVES 10

GRUYÈRE BISQUE

½ CUP UNSALTED BUTTER
½ CUP SMALL-DICE ONION
½ CUP SMALL-DICE CELERY
⅓ CUP ALL-PURPOSE FLOUR
2 CUPS CHICKEN STOCK
2 CUPS MILK
3 CUPS GRATED GRUYÈRE CHEESE
2 CUPS HEAVY CREAM
KOSHER SALT, TO TASTE
GROUND WHITE PEPPER, TO TASTE
FRESH CHIVES, MINCED, TO GARNISH

1. In a stockpot, melt the butter over medium heat.
2. Saute onion and celery for 10 minutes.
3. Add flour and stir to form roux. Cook mixture for several minutes (but do not burn).
4. Stir in chicken stock and then milk and whip until smooth. Turn heat to low and bring to a simmer.
5. Once mixture begins to thicken, add Gruyère cheese. Continue to simmer and work bisque with a whip to achieve smooth consistency. A stick blender can be a handy tool for these types of soups.
6. Finish with heavy cream and adjust seasoning to taste with salt and pepper. The consistency can be adjusted with stock or milk as needed. Use fresh minced chives for garnish once the dish is portioned for service.

CARAMELIZED ONION FLATBREAD

5 FLATBREAD (TANDOORI NAAN OR PITA FLATS, NOT POCKETS)
¼ CUP UNSALTED BUTTER
1½ CUPS FINE-JULIENNE RED ONION
1½ CUPS FINE-JULIENNE VIDALIA ONION
1 CUP PEELED PEARL ONIONS
1 CUP FINE-JULIENNE LEEKS
2 TABLESPOONS MINCED GARLIC
2 CUPS RED WINE
1 CUP GRANULATED SUGAR
1 TABLESPOON MINCED FRESH THYME
½ CUP CHÈVRE GOAT CHEESE
KOSHER SALT, TO TASTE
GROUND BLACK PEPPER, TO TASTE

1. Preheat oven to 375 degrees.
2. Toast flatbread in oven for 10 minutes, remove, and allow to cool to room temperature.

THIS DISH TRULY CELEBRATES THE ONION IN ALL OF ITS VARIOUS TEXTURES, AROMAS, AND FLAVORS.

reverse french onion soup
GRUYÈRE BISQUE, CARAMELIZED ONION FLATBREAD, FRIZZLED LEEKS, CHIVE OIL

3. In a large skillet over medium-high heat, caramelize the red onion in some of the butter. It is important to use small batches to maintain your product-to-hot surface ratio. Repeat the process for each type of onion, keeping them separate once finished. Reserve a small amount of each type of onion.
4. Place the remaining onions (all types) in a saucepan and then add the minced garlic, red wine, sugar, and half of the fresh thyme.
5. Allow mixture to reduce over low heat until jam-like consistency is achieved.
6. Turn oven down to 300 degrees.
7. Spread onion jam generously over pre-baked flatbread.
8. Garnish with reserved caramelized onions of each type, crumbled chèvre, and remainder of fresh thyme.
9. Season to taste with salt and pepper, place flatbread on a baking sheet, and warm in the oven for 15 minutes.

FRIZZLED LEEKS

4 CUPS CANOLA OIL
3 CUPS SUPERFINE-JULIENNE LEEKS
KOSHER SALT, TO TASTE

1. In a tall saucepan, bring canola oil to medium-low heat\ (275 degrees).
2. Add leeks and allow them to simmer/fry until crisp (about 20 minutes).
3. Strain the leeks and lightly season to taste with salt. Frying at a low temperature will ensure the correct color and texture in the finished product.

CHIVE OIL

½ CUP CHOPPED CHIVES
½ CUP CANOLA OIL
KOSHER SALT, TO TASTE

1. In a blender or with a stick blender, pulse chives and oil together and then season to taste with salt.
2. Refrigerate at least 12 hours to allow flavors to merry. Strain oil if desired. (As a general rule, always refrigerate infused oils.)

ASSEMBLY: Ladle 6 ounces of the bisque into an appropriate vessel with a base plate large enough to accommodate the flatbread. Top the soup with minced chives. Cut the flatbread into 10 servings and then place the pieces onto plates next to the soup. Drizzle with chive oil and garnish the flatbread with a ball of the frizzled leeks.

paella

ROASTED CHICKEN LEG, SEARED SCALLOPS & SHRIMP, WINE-STEAMED MUSSELS & CLAMS, CHORIZO SAUSAGE, ISRAELI COUSCOUS, SAFFRON BEURRE BLANC

TRADITIONAL PAELLA IS A DISH MADE BY PUTTING A BUNCH of ingredients together in a pan and then letting them cook. My version of paella pushes you to pay attention to every component. We want the chicken to be perfectly roasted. We want the scallops and shrimp to be perfectly pan-seared. We want the sausage to be grilled. We're using couscous instead of rice, which adds a little pop to the dish when you eat it. Each ingredient gets the respect and admiration it deserves.

paella
ROASTED CHICKEN LEG, SEARED SCALLOPS & SHRIMP, WINE-STEAMED MUSSELS & CLAMS, CHORIZO SAUSAGE, ISRAELI COUSCOUS, SAFFRON BEURRE BLANC
SERVES 8

ISRAELI COUSCOUS

4 SLICES THICK-CUT BACON, SMALL DICE
1/4 CUP BRUNOISE RED ONION*
1/2 CUP BRUNOISE RED PEPPER*
1 CUP GREEN PEAS (YOUNG)
3/4 CUP BRUNOISE ROMA TOMATO, FLESH ONLY (NO SEEDS)*
1/4 CUP UNSALTED BUTTER
1/2 CUP BRUNOISE SHALLOT*
1 TABLESPOON MINCED GARLIC
3 CUPS ISRAELI COUSCOUS
2 FRESH BAY LEAVES
1/2 TEASPOON CRUSHED SAFFRON
1 3/4 CUPS CHICKEN STOCK
2 CUPS SEAFOOD STOCK
SEA SALT, TO TASTE
FRESHLY GROUND BLACK PEPPER, TO TASTE
1 TABLESPOON MINCED CHIVES

1. In a large skillet over medium heat, render bacon until crisp.
2. Add red onion and saute until it just begins to caramelize.
3. Add red pepper and peas and saute for 3 minutes; stir in Roma tomatoes and remove from heat. Allow flavors to marry. Set aside until called for.
4. Melt butter in a heavy saucepan over medium heat.
5. Add shallots and garlic and saute for about five minutes.
6. Add couscous and bay leaves and lightly toast couscous, stirring often (about 5 minutes).
7. Add saffron, chicken stock, and seafood stock and then bring to a boil.
8. Reduce heat to low; cover and simmer until couscous is just tender and liquid is nearly absorbed (about 8 minutes).
9. Remove from heat and then gently stir in bacon and vegetable mixture.
10. Adjust flavor to taste with sea salt and pepper and then garnish with minced chives. Keep warm for service.

SAFFRON BEURRE BLANC

1/2 CUP DRY WHITE WINE
2 TABLESPOONS ROUGHLY CHOPPED SHALLOTS
10 SAFFRON THREADS
1/3 CUP HEAVY WHIPPING CREAM
1 CUP UNSALTED BUTTER (CUT INTO TABLESPOON-SIZE PIECES AND CHILLED)
SEA SALT, TO TASTE
GROUND WHITE PEPPER, TO TASTE

1. Boil wine, shallots, and saffron in a heavy medium sauce pan over medium-high heat until liquid is reduced to about 2 tablespoons (about five minutes).
2. Add cream and bring to a boil for about 1 minute.
3. Reduce heat to low and add a few pieces of butter, whisking constantly. Add the remaining butter a few pieces at a time once previous pieces have melted and are incorporated. Remove pan from heat occasionally if needed to cool mixture.
4. Once all butter is incorporated, remove sauce from heat and season to taste with salt and pepper.
5. Pass the sauce through a fine sieve at least once and discard what doesn't go through sieve. Sauce should be velvety and beautiful saffron gold in color.

FOR PAELLA GARNISHES

8 CHICKEN DRUMETTES, FRENCHED
SEA SALT, TO TASTE
FRESH GROUND BLACK PEPPER, TO TASTE
2 TABLESPOONS FINELY CHOPPED FRESH THYME
2 TABLESPOONS OLIVE OIL
8 OUNCES CHORIZO
8 U10 SCALLOPS**
16 21/25 CT. SHRIMP, PEELED AND DEVEINED**
16 FRESH CHERRYSTONE CLAMS
16 FRESH GREEN LIP MUSSELS
½ CUP WHITE WINE

1. Preheat oven to 250 degrees.
2. Season chicken drumettes with salt, pepper, and 1 tablespoon of the thyme.
3. Bring a large heavy skillet to medium heat with oil and brown the drumettes on all sides.
4. Transport the chicken to a baking sheet and place in the oven to finish cooking (about 10-15 minutes).
5. Meanwhile, using the same skillet, render the chorizo sausage leaving it in the casing to be served in slices.
6. Place chorizo in the oven with the chicken to finish if needed, otherwise set aside.
7. Season the scallops and shrimp to taste with sea salt and saute in the same skillet used for the chicken and sausage, using the same oil.
8. Cook the scallops and shrimp until golden brown in color, but not finished.
9. Remove them from heat to rest and return momentarily.
10. Now, add the clams and mussels to the same skillet.
11. Add the white wine and cover the pan. Let the clams and mussels steam for approximately 3-4 minutes.
12. Return the scallops and shrimp to the pan and sprinkle with the remaining thyme. Season to taste with salt and pepper. The seafood should just finish as the chicken finishes in the oven.

ASSEMBLY: Timing is everything in this concept of deconstructing paella. The advantage to cooking paella all together is flavor building, but the disadvantage can be the over-cooking of certain ingredients. This entire dish is put together in a specific way to highlight what is perfect about the dish as a whole. Concentrating on perfection throughout all of the individual ingredients is what makes this dish extremely memorable. Timing is crucial to this type of concept.

Choose a vessel that allows plenty of plating space. Spoon a small amount of couscous onto the center. Work the seafood, chicken, and sausage into and around the couscous. Ladle the beurre blanc over and around the dish.

*A "brunoise" cut refers to cutting the ingredient first into ⅛-inch matchsticks and then into ⅛-inch cubes.

**This number indicates how the items are sized when they are packed, which means that there is approximately that number of items per one pound.

WINE
RIOJA (RED) OR ALBARINO (WHITE). From northeastern Spain, Rioja wines display notes of dark cherry and tobacco, with subtle vanilla and spice from oak barrels. The light spicy finish and tannic notes will compliment the chorizo and saffron spices while accentuating the roasted chicken. Crisp and fragrant notes of flowers, pears, and tropical fruit dominate the popular Spanish white. Its acidity and dry finish makes it a great pairing for nearly all shellfish and spicy foods.

BEER
DORTMUNDER LAGER. Golden hues and dry, bready maltiness make up the profile of this classic German lager. Clean and light on the palate, with moderate bitterness, these beers make for great accompaniments to poultry and seafood. In the summer months, seek out the Two Brothers Brewing Co. Dog Days of Summer Dortmunder Lager from Warrenville, Illinois, a particularly appropriate pairing with this dish.

winter bbq

GRILLED ANTELOPE CHOP, CRANBERRY BARBECUE SAUCE, PEAR & FENNEL SLAW,
ROSEMARY WHITE BEAN CASSOULET, SWEET POTATO CHIPS

SUMMER IS THE SEASON FOR BARBECUE, RIGHT?

Yes—but. I wanted to challenge that traditional notion by looking at barbecue from the perspective of winter. In my mind, the essential elements of a barbecue cookout are meat, potato chips, slaw, and baked beans. This dish has all of those components, but with a different seasonal character. Our meat is antelope, and game meats certainly have a wintertime feel. Instead of a tomato-based sauce, this sauce uses cranberry, another cold-weather ingredient. Instead of baked beans, we're making braised white beans with rosemary, the slaw includes late-season pears rather than cabbage, and our chips are made from sweet potatoes.

winter bbq
GRILLED ANTELOPE CHOP, CRANBERRY BARBECUE SAUCE, PEAR & FENNEL SLAW, ROSEMARY WHITE BEAN CASSOULET, SWEET POTATO CHIPS
SERVES 10

ROSEMARY WHITE BEAN CASSOULET

6 APPLE WOOD BACON SLICES, SMALL DICE
1 MEDIUM ONION, BRUNOISE*
1 POUND DRIED NAVY BEANS, SOAKED OVERNIGHT
  AND DRAINED
2 CUPS VEGETABLE OR CHICKEN STOCK
1 TABLESPOON DIJON MUSTARD
3/4 CUP PACKED BROWN SUGAR
1 TABLESPOON FINELY CHOPPED ROSEMARY
KOSHER SALT, TO TASTE
GROUND BLACK PEPPER, TO TASTE

1. Preheat oven to 350 degrees.
2. In a large saucepan over medium heat, render the bacon until crisp.
3. Add onion and saute for 5 minutes until transparent, but not caramelized.
4. Add beans, stock, mustard, and brown sugar, and then bring to a simmer.
5. Cover and place in oven and bake for 45 minutes, until beans are tender and most of the liquid is absorbed.
6. Finish with fresh rosemary, salt, and pepper.

PEAR & FENNEL SLAW

DRESSING

2 TEASPOONS FENNEL SEEDS
2 TEASPOONS ANISE SEEDS
1/2 CUP MAYONNAISE
1/4 CUP CHAMPAGNE VINEGAR
1/4 CUP GRANULATED SUGAR
KOSHER SALT, TO TASTE
FRESHLY GROUND WHITE PEPPER, TO TASTE

1. Toast fennel and anise seeds in a dry heavy skillet over medium heat, shaking occasionally, until lightly browned, then cool.
2. Using a coffee grinder, grind seeds together.
3. In a mixing bowl, whisk together ground seeds with remaining ingredients.

SLAW

2 MEDIUM-SIZE FENNEL BULBS, STALKS REMOVED AND
  DISCARDED (BUT RESERVE FRONDS)
1 TABLESPOON FRESH LEMON JUICE
3 RED PEARS, CORED AND JULIENNED
1/2 CUP FINELY JULIENNED RED ONION
DRESSING (SEE RECIPE AT LEFT)

1. Halve fennel bulbs lengthwise, then cut out and discard cores.
2. Thinly slice fennel crosswise on a mandoline and toss with lemon juice in a large bowl.
3. Finely chop enough fennel fronds to measure 1/8 cup and add to sliced fennel.
4. Add remaining ingredients and toss with enough dressing to lightly coat. Chill, covered, for at least 1 hour to allow flavors to fully develop.

SWEET POTATO CHIPS

4 SWEET POTATOES, PEELED (ABOUT 3 POUNDS)
CANOLA OIL, FOR DEEP-FRYING
COARSE SALT, TO TASTE

1. With a mandoline, cut potatoes into 1/16-inch slices and then place them in cool water for 30 minutes to leech out the starch.
2. Drain off the water and pat the slices dry with paper towels.
3. In a deep fryer or pot, bring canola oil to 370 degrees.
4. Fry the potato slices in small batches, turning them, until they are golden and crisp (about 2 minutes). Visually, the bubbles from frying will nearly subside.
5. Transfer the chips with a slotted spoon or tongs to a paper towel-lined pan to drain and then season to taste with salt.

CRANBERRY BARBECUE SAUCE

1/2 CUP BROWN SUGAR
2 CUPS FRESH CRANBERRIES
1/2 CUP MAPLE SYRUP
1 1/2 CUPS CRAN-RASPBERRY JUICE
2 TABLESPOONS DIJON MUSTARD
1 TEASPOON LIQUID SMOKE
1 TABLESPOON CHILI POWDER
2 TEASPOONS GROUND CUMIN
1/4 TEASPOON GROUND BLACK PEPPER
KOSHER SALT, TO TASTE

1. Place all ingredients in a saucepan and bring to a boil.
2. Reduce heat and simmer slowly for 1 hour.
3. Puree sauce until smooth and then strain.
4. Return sauce to heat and continue reducing until it reaches desired consistency.
5. Season to taste with salt.

GRILLED ANTELOPE CHOPS

VEGETABLE OIL, AS NEEDED
10 5- TO 6-OUNCE CENTER-CUT ANTELOPE CHOPS,
  FRENCHED**
2 TABLESPOONS GRANULATED SUGAR
2 TABLESPOONS CHILI POWDER
3 TEASPOONS KOSHER SALT
2 TEASPOONS DRY MUSTARD
2 TEASPOONS GRANULATED GARLIC
2 TEASPOONS GROUND BLACK PEPPER
1 TEASPOON CHIPOTLE CHILI POWDER
3 TEASPOONS GROUND CUMIN
CRANBERRY BARBECUE SAUCE (RECIPE AT LEFT)

1. Preheat grill with a clean rack to medium-high heat.
2. Oil grill rack with a towel.
3. In a medium bowl, add all dry ingredients and mix well.
4. Rub antelope chops generously with spice rub.
5. Cover bones with foil if needed to prevent burning.
6. Grill chops on all sides (approximately 6 minutes per side).
7. Remove chops when they reach 130 degrees internal temperature.
8. Rest chops for 5-8 minutes before serving.
9. Brush generously with the Cranberry Barbecue Sauce.

ASSEMBLY: Bare in mind that this is a tasting experience that plays with all the popular flavors of summertime BBQ, but with a winter feel and influence. Choose a vessel that will allow you to "lay out" this experience, leaving plenty of room for the diner to work through it. A beautiful clean-line approach is stunning, to say the least. Enjoy!

*A "brunoise" cut refers to cutting the ingredient first into 1/8-inch matchsticks and then into 1/8-inch cubes.

**"Frenched" is a butcher's term referring to the exposed bones of the cut of meat. The bones add more flavor and tenderness to the meat and, after they are finished cooking, they are good for presentation purposes.

WINE
SHIRAZ. Deep dark and inky in color, with intense notes of peppered spice and dark ripe fruits, the Australian Shirazes carry a full-bodied mouth feel and a long, warming finish. The Barossa Valley of southern Australia has the perfect climate to grow these luscious and intensely dark grapes.

BEER
PORTER. Very dark and robust, porters offer notes of chocolate, coffee, caramel, and dark fruits, and are the perfect match for barbecue of all sorts because they contrast the sweet and tangy flavors of the sauce and compliment the grilled notes of the meat.

lamb osso bucco
BRAISED LAMB SHANK, MINT GREMOLATA, LENTILS, RED ONION MARMALADE
SERVES 10

BRAISED LAMB SHANK

10 1 1/2-TO 2-INCH-THICK LAMB LEG STEAKS, CUT "OSSO BUCCO STYLE" ON A BAND SAW (ASK YOUR BUTCHER)
1 TABLESPOON KOSHER SALT
GROUND BLACK PEPPER, TO TASTE
1 CUP WONDRA FLOUR
ABOUT 1/4 CUP CANOLA OIL
2 SHALLOTS, COARSELY CHOPPED
4 WHOLE CLOVES
1/2 CUP DRY WHITE WINE
1/2 CUP RED WINE
2 SPRIGS FRESH ROSEMARY
2 SPRIGS FRESH THYME
5 CLOVES GARLIC, FINELY CHOPPED

1. Preheat oven to 350 degree.
2. Pat lamb shanks dry.
3. Season lamb with salt and pepper.
4. Dredge in flour and pat off excess flour.
5. In large heavy skillet over moderately high heat, heat 1 tablespoon of the oil until it is hot but not smoking. Working in batches, sear shanks, turning occasionally, until brown on all sides (about 5 minutes per batch). Transfer as browned to a large roasting pan. Do not clean fat from skillet.
6. Lower heat to moderate and then add shallots and cloves, then saute until shallots are soft (about 8 minutes).
7. Whisk in wine, rosemary, thyme, garlic, and salt, then raise heat and bring to a boil.
8. Pour mixture over shanks, cover tightly with foil, and then braise in the middle of the oven until meat is very tender (about 2 1/2-3 hours.
9. Transfer shanks gently to baking sheet and cover loosely with foil. Keep warm.
10. Pour braising liquid through fine-mesh strainer into medium-heavy saucepan, pressing on the solids with the back of a spoon. Skim fat from sauce if needed.
11. Place saucepan over moderately high heat and bring to boil, then lower heat and simmer, uncovered, until sauce is reduced by half (about 25 minutes). Keep sauce warm for assembly.

MINT GREMOLATA

3 TABLESPOONS CHOPPED FRESH MINT
2 TEASPOONS FINELY MINCED GARLIC
1 TEASPOON GRATED LIME ZEST
1 TEASPOON GRATED LEMON ZEST

1. Combine all ingredients on a cutting board and continue to chop together with a knife until ingredients are well blended.

STEWED LENTILS AND PUREE

1 TABLESPOON VEGETABLE OIL
3/4 CUP BRUNOISE ONION*
3 LARGE GARLIC CLOVES, MINCED
1/2 CUP BRUNOISE CELERY*
1 POUND GREEN LENTILS
6 CUPS CHICKEN STOCK
2 FRESH BAY LEAVES
3 TABLESPOONS BUTTER
1 TABLESPOON FINELY CHOPPED PARSLEY
SALT AND PEPPER, TO TASTE

1. Heat oil in heavy large pot over medium-high heat.
2. Add onion, garlic, and celery and then saute until tender (about 5 minutes).
3. Add lentils, stock, and bay leaves; bring to boil.
4. Reduce heat to medium-low and simmer until lentils are tender (about 45 minutes or less).
5. Strain lentils, reserving cooking liquid and removing bay leaves.
6. Divide lentils into half. Season half with salt and pepper and keep warm.
7. In a food processor, blend the other half of the lentils, incorporating some of the reserved cooking liquid to adjust the texture to ribbon-like consistency.**
8. Add some unsalted butter and the fresh parsley. Adjust seasoning and continue pureeing until very smooth. Keep warm.

RED ONION MARMALADE

1 1/2 TABLESPOONS BUTTER, UNSALTED
3 CUPS THINLY JULIENNED RED ONIONS (ABOUT 3 POUNDS)
1/2 CUP DARK BROWN SUGAR, PACKED
1/8 CUP RED WINE VINEGAR
1/2 CUP RED WINE
1/4 CUP DRY SHERRY
KOSHER SALT, TO TASTE
GROUND BLACK PEPPER, TO TASTE

1. Melt butter in a heavy large pot over medium heat.
2. Add onions and cook until onions are tender, stirring occasionally (about 30 minutes).
3. Add brown sugar, vinegar, and wine. Cook uncovered until onions are very tender and mixture is thick, stirring frequently (about 20 minutes).
4. Add sherry and continue cooking until mixture is very thick and dark, stirring frequently.
5. Season to taste with salt and pepper. Cool completely. (Can be prepared 4 days ahead. Cover and refrigerate.)

ASSEMBLY: Remember to leave room on the plate, because the diner is probably going to be cutting and working around a bone in the osso bucco. Spoon on some of the lentil puree and scatter an artful pile of the braised lentils onto the plate, then place a braised lamb shank in the center. Garnish with mint gremolata and the red onion marmalade. Drizzle on the braising reduction and serve.

*A "brunoise" cut refers to cutting the ingredient first into ¹/₈-inch matchsticks and then into ¹/₈-inch cubes.

**"Ribbon" is a cooking term meaning that when the spoon or whisk is lifted, the batter falls slowly back onto the surface of the mixture, forming a ribbon-like pattern that, after a few seconds, sinks back into the batter.

WINE
MERLOT. A classic pairing with lamb, Merlots are softer, fruitier, and mature faster than Cabernet Sauvignon, yet display similar characteristics of black currant, mint, cherry, and tobacco. Shafer Winery from Napa Valley produces some of the finest Merlots in the world and would offer the ultimate pairing.

BEER
BROWN ALE. Lighter in body than a porter but with common notes of chocolate and coffee, brown ales prove to be a perfect paring for game meats and offer a great balance between hops and caramel malts, with a slight fruity note on the finish. Both American and British brown ales offer the malty backbone needed to compliment this dish.

dessert sushi
BANANA NORI, VANILLA BEAN RICE PUDDING, MANGO/PAPAYA/PLUM, WASABI GREEN APPLE SORBET, CANDIED GINGER, MISO BUTTERSCOTCH

SERVES 10

DRIED BANANA SHEETS

This is our dessert sushi "nori," if you will.

4 RIPE BANANAS

1. To make banana sheets, simply blend the bananas in a food processor until smooth, then spread the mixture thinly and evenly onto Teflex sheets.*
2. Dehydrate at 110 degrees until no longer sticky to the touch (about 2-3 hours).
3. You should be able to peel the sheets easily from the Teflex and cut to desired size with scissors or a knife.

dessert sushi
BANANA NORI, VANILLA BEAN RICE PUDDING, MANGO/PAPAYA/PLUM,
WASABI GREEN APPLE SORBET, CANDIED GINGER, MISO BUTTERSCOTCH

VANILLA BEAN RICE PUDDING

1 1/2 CUPS WATER
3/4 CUP SUSHI RICE
1/4 TEASPOON KOSHER SALT
2 CUPS WHOLE MILK
1 CUP HEAVY WHIPPING CREAM
1/2 CUP GRANULATED SUGAR
1 VANILLA BEAN, SPLIT LENGTHWISE

1. Bring water, rice, and salt to simmer in a heavy large saucepan over medium-high heat. Reduce heat to low; cover. Simmer until water is absorbed (about 10 minutes).
2. Add milk, cream, and sugar.
3. Scrape in seeds from vanilla been; add bean. Increase heat to medium; cook uncovered until rice is tender and mixture thickens slightly to a soft, creamy texture, stirring occasionally (about 35 minutes).
4. Remove pudding from heat and discard vanilla bean. Allow to cool to room temperature.

WASABI GREEN APPLE SORBET

2 CUPS CLEAR APPLE JUICE
3 GRANNY SMITH APPLES (ABOUT 1 1/2 POUNDS), PEELED AND
   CUT INTO 1/2-INCH PIECES
1 TABLESPOON FRESH LEMON JUICE
3 TABLESPOONS GRANULATED SUGAR
1 TEASPOON WASABI POWDER
PINCH OF KOSHER SALT

1. In large saucepan combine all ingredients and simmer, uncovered (10 minutes, or until apples are very tender).
2. Strain mixture through a sieve into a blender and then add half of the solids in sieve to a blender, discarding the remaining solids. Puree apple mixture and chill until cold.
3. Freeze sorbet in an ice cream maker. Sorbet may be made 1 week ahead. Wasabi may be adjusted depending on preference of heat.

CANDIED GINGER

You don't need a candy thermometer to make this. Simply keep an eye on the pot, and when the liquid is the consistency of thin honey, it's done and ready to go.

1/2 POUND FRESH GINGER, PEELED
2 CUPS GRANULATED SUGAR, PLUS ADDITIONAL SUGAR FOR
   COATING THE GINGER SLICE (IF DESIRED)
2 CUPS WATER
PINCH OF KOSHER SALT

1. Slice the ginger as thinly as possible. It can't be too thin, so use a sharp knife or a mandoline.
2. Put the ginger slices in a non-reactive pot, cover with water and bring to a boil. Reduce heat and let ginger simmer for 10 minutes. Drain and repeat one more time.
3. Mix the sugar and water in the pot, along with a pinch of salt and the ginger slices, and cook until the temperature reaches 225 degrees.
4. Drain very well and toss in more granulated sugar (if desired).
5. Shake off excess sugar and spread the ginger slices on a cooling rack overnight, until they are somewhat dry. Store at room temperature.

MISO BUTTERSCOTCH

3/4 CUP BROWN SUGAR
1/2 CUP CORN SYRUP
2 TABLESPOONS UNSALTED BUTTER
1 CUP HEAVY WHIPPING CREAM
6 TABLESPOONS WHITE MISO PASTE

1. In a medium saucepan over medium heat, add sugar, corn syrup, butter, and heavy cream; simmer until it is thick (about 10 minutes).
2. Allow to cool at room temperature and blend in miso paste.

SUSHI ROLLS

DRIED "NORI" BANANA SHEETS, CUT INTO 3-BY-8-INCH
   RECTANGLES (RECIPE ON PREVIOUS PAGE)
MANGOS, PAPAYA, AND/OR PLUMS, CUT INTO BATONETTES OR
   JULIENNED AND FINELY SLICED
GREEN APPLE, THINLY SLICED
VANILLA BEAN RICE PUDDING (COOL)
BLACKBERRIES OR RASPBERRIES (FRESH)

Using the same techniques for rolling traditional sushi, as well as the same equipment (such as a sushi mat) in this recipe is something to bear in mind. The rice pudding can be used inside or outside of the "nori." Quenelles** of the rice pudding are also appropriate, which may be topped with finely sliced fruit. Using the sushi mat, lay down the banana sheet horizontally and top with a thin layer of rice pudding. There should be a small amount of banana sheet showing on the top

and bottom. Next, place the batonettes or julienne of a selected fruit down the center and on top of the rice pudding. Finally, tightly roll the sushi into a log so that the fruit is directly down the center, surrounded by rice pudding and then banana sheet. Dampen your finger in a little water and brush it over the exposed flap for a secured seal. Keep each roll to just one type of fruit in the center, but repeat this process with an assortment of rolls. Refrigerate rolls until ready to slice and present. For blackberry or raspberry garnish, cutting the berries in half is just fine; or, if you want a challenge and your berries are really nice, you can make a bit of caviar by using a small, sharp knife to break down the berries one tiny section at a time. Look closely at the berry and you will see that each berry is made up of hundreds of tiny seed-like blossoms. Using your knife, carefully work through the berry taking it apart. Use this "caviar" to garnish some of your rolls.

ASSEMBLY: I really like to have this presentation resemble traditional sushi. A nice sushi block or Asian-style vessel works great. You definitely want something a little flat for spreading it out a bit. The miso butterscotch can be drizzled or spooned across the vessel. Lay out your selection of various rolls across the plate. It may be wise to scoop your sorbet ahead and also serve it in a small frozen vessel that can be built into the presentation. The fine slices of green apple make a terrific fence against the back of the sorbet. Garnish the dish with candied ginger. This is a dish that is truly concept-driven. The creativity in flavors and presentation are endless. For those of you who enjoy preparing sushi, you will have a great deal of fun playing with this idea.

*Teflex is a brand of nonstick sheeting used in dehydrators.

**"Quenelles" are little football-shaped scoops formed by working a formable ingredient in and out of two spoons.

WINE
GERMAN REISLING. Preferably Spatlese in style, these medium-bodied, sweet, late-harvest whites exude notes of honey and stone fruits such as peach and apricot, with a slight minerality in the finish.

BEER
GINGER BEER. Light and refreshing, with distinct aromas of flowers and ginger, these ales offer a crisp mouthfeel with light ginger spice. The traditional ginger beer is Japan's Hitachino Nest Real Ginger Ale. A summer offering from Colorado that would work well with this concept is Good JuJu Ginger from Left Hand Brewing Company.

DESSERT SUSHI IS A CONCEPT-DRIVEN DISH. HAVE FUN PLAYING WITH THE IDEA.

RESOURCES

Broken Arrow Ranch
*Specializes in wild game,
including boar, antelope, venison
and elk.*

3296 Junction Highway
Ingram, TX 78205
800-962-4263
www.brokenarrowranch.com

**The Emporium at
Joseph Decuis**
*Specializes in American
Wagyu beef.*

191 North Main Street
Roanoke, IN 46783
260-672-1715
info@josephdecuis.com
www.josephdecuis.com

JB Prince
*Specializes in professional chef
tools and equipment.*

36 East 31st Street
New York, NY 10016
800-473-0577
www.jbprince.com

Michigan Venison Company
*Supplies all-natural, wild-
harvested whitetail venison from
Michigan's North Woods.*

PO Box 4153
Traverse City, MI 49685
http://michiganvenison.foodzie.com/
info@michiganvenison.com

ACKNOWLEDGMENTS. My heartfelt gratitude goes out to **Ryan Pierce** for his dedication, time, and significant work in creating beer and wine pairings, as well as playing a vital role with The Personal Palate; to **Albert Schlaepfer** for his help in organizing the recipes in the book; to **Bryan Ferreria** and **Pat Whetstone** for taking time to be part of the photographed crew within this book, as well as helping so very often with events over the last several years; to my dear friend **Allen Gustin** for playing a vital role in my life as a chef, mentor and friend; to **Gregg McQuillan** for always challenging me to be better at food and beverage, period. Additional thanks go to the following people for their hard work during the beginning years of my business: **Reinier Blok** and **Brad Miller**. I would also like to thank my clients from past, present and future, whose desire for wonderful food experiences keeps me challenged to deliver them. I also owe a debt of gratitude to **Steelite**, which provided a large amount of china for extraordinary presentations, to **Ursula David Homes (www.ursuladavidhomes.com)** and **Form + Function**, which provided lovely interiors and furniture for some of the photo shoots in the book, and to models **Zoe Moore**, **Kirsten Weber**, and **Artur Silva** for appearing in the photos.